The Project Management Play Book

It's a Team Sport

Keith E. Wilson

kwilson@pmpractice.com

ISBN 0-7414-4639-1

Published by:

INFINITY
PUBLISHING.COM

1094 New DeHaven Street, Suite 100
West Conshohocken, PA 19428-2713
Info@buybooksontheweb.com
www.buybooksontheweb.com
Toll-free (877) BUY BOOK
Local Phone (610) 941-9999
Fax (610) 941-9959

Printed in the United States of America

Printed on Recycled Paper

Published December 2008

Table of Contents

Foreword

During my twenty-five years in the project management profession, I have experienced numerous challenges in managing projects and programs in the following industries: government (federal and local), construction, oil and gas and high technology. I found the principles of the Project Management Institute (PMI®) and the American Society for the Advancement of Project Management (ASAPM®) very effective. I also enjoyed the fortune of meeting several Subject Matter Experts (SMEs).

Keith Wilson is one of those SMEs. We stayed in touch since that first day he slammed down a hockey puck on the podium to illustrate his point. He definitely earned everyone's attention as he was explaining how project management is like winning a hockey game! Effective project management requires teamwork (communications), players (project team), playbook (project plan), coach (project manager), team owner (project sponsor), points (deliverables) and most importantly the fans (client users).

Keith's book is a pleasure to read because he uses sports to illustrate basic project management principles. This learning technique keeps the reader hooked and wanting to read the next chapter.

BAM! BANG! SLAP! GOAL!!! The Project Management Playbook – It's a Team Sport is the winning coach's personal playbook for project management success. If you want to score project management points, enjoy this book. **Matt Piazza, MBA, PMP (#640) piazzam@deltasol.net**

Acknowledgments

I would like to extend a special thanks to Robert Happy, one of my fellow executives at PM Practice and business partner since 1990. Over the years we have contributed to a Project Management Process manual that has had many iterations and versions. We have used it in training thousands of people and that manual has been the basis of this book. All interpretations or errors are solely my responsibility.

Also thanks to other PM Practice executives: Sean Creaghan the guy that keeps us all glued together, James Bulmer and David Blair project management technical geniuses. James first taught me how to teach project management, and David was also one of the Symantec executives that purchased Time Line Solution with Robert, two others and myself.

I give special thanks to my editors Barbara Kari (aka my Mother), AnnMarie Handsel and David Blair. My sincere appreciation and thanks to Matt Piazza who is a well respected career Project Management Professional, with years of Project Management experience. He was very kind to review and make recommendations for the book.

This book is dedicated to my children, Maverick and Sky Wilson.

In preparing this book, I put myself in your shoes; a person trying to expand their skills and tools to manage projects. I developed a list of 5 questions that I thought you might ask before starting the core of this book, including:

1. Who is Keith Wilson and what is the Project Management Practice?
2. Why another project management book?
3. What is the game plan?
4. What are the benefits to my organization?
5. Are supporting tools or forms offered with the play book?

Let's start by answering these questions as a great way to begin working together!

Who is Keith Wilson (kwilson@pmpractice.com)?

I've been a consultant since 1986 and started my consulting career in my home town of Ottawa, Ontario, Canada. I opened my first consulting company in 1988 when we launched a software application called *"The Customer Manager"*. In 1995, Robert Happy and I sold our Canadian consulting company and moved to California to become Vice-Presidents with *Symantec*. Ten months later we bought *Time Line*, a project management software solution from Symantec and formed a new company called *Time Line Solutions Corp*.

We quickly realized that we were going head-to-head with this guy named Bill and it didn't make sense to compete against Microsoft®. We repositioned our company to be the **Project Management Practice Inc,** specializing in Project Management training and consulting.

In summary, my background includes 25 years of successful management and consulting experience, specializing in project management, training, and consulting across many industries. In addition to a Diploma in Business Administration, I have a Bachelor Degree in Commerce (with Honors), a Masters in Business Administration and am a certified trainer in: FranklinCovey Project Management, "We Sell with the Best", a sales skills course modeled after the IBM and Xerox sales methodologies, and Oracle. My teaching has included e-Business Project Management at the British Columbia Institute of Technology (College). I am fortunate to be well known for my public speaking enthusiasm and have been a welcome facilitator at numerous fortune 500 companies, universities, and associations throughout North America, Europe and Asia. I have also managed complex, multi-million dollar projects and provided in-depth business analysis to many different industries, ranging from high technology to retail.

My Partial Client List

Military	Hi Tech	Telecom/Utilities	Government
US Marines	Microsoft	Verizon	Social Security
US Air force	Symantec	Sprint PCS	Administration
US Navy	Oracle	ACS	State- North Carolina, and
Canadian Armed Force	Prologic	GCI	Alaska
Police	(Banking Software)	Union Telephone	Canada Post
RCMP	Image Power	Cisco	Federal Government
Illinois State Police	(Image compression)	Nokia	Canadian Dept. of Justice
Manufacturing	Newlix	Golden Valley Electric	Human Resources
Ingersoll Rand	(Linux Software)	**Oil and Gas**	Development Canada
Knauf Fiber Glass	Softwex Technologies	ExxonMobil	Environment Canada
PrintPack	(Multimedia software)	Alyeska	Canadian Achieves
Butler Mfg.	Whetstone Technologies	Williams	Alberta Learning
Consulting	(Image software)	Joint Alaska Pipeline	Alberta Aboriginal Affairs
TBM	Relay	Tesco	Alberta Environment
(Productivity Effectiveness)	(Gaming Software)	McDermott	City -Richmond Virginia
FranklinCovey	Clever Devices	**Transportation**	Galveston County
Deloitte	(Transportation SW)	Cunard Cruise Lines	Harris County
MCO (HR)	AMIs (Semiconductor)	Boeing	CMHC
Priority Management	Honeywell	Kenworth	Privy Council
E&Y	Mindjet	**Pharmaceutical**	**Automotive**
ASM Research	McAfee	Pfizer	General Motors
Design and Construction	Keystone Learning	**Associations**	Unit Parts
KDA (Banks and Credit	**Pulp and Paper**	Canadian Library	John Deere
Unions)	Fletcher Challenge Canada	Association	Volvo
LNR	**Food and Restaurant**	Canadian Wood Council	American Honda
Education	Fat Alberts and Ralph's	Indian Desert River Band	Paccar/Kenworth
Carleton University	Dannon yogurt	American Quarter Horse	**Retail**
Ottawa University	Coke-a-Cola	Association	Tiffany and Company
UBC	**Legal**	Cherokee Nation Ent.	The Bay
BCIT	With out Prejudice	**Entertainment**	Macys
PPI on Course	Alternative Dispute	Viacom/MTV	Circuit City
Ivy Training Center	Resolution	**Airlines**	
U of Alaska	**Health Care Systems**	AA	
Financial	Argus	**Media/PR**	
Federal Home Loan Bank	Medidata	Seattle Times	
Raymond James	Landacorp	The Gallatin Group	
WAMU	CYTYC		
Jefferies & Co.			

What is the Project Management Practice Inc.?

We are a Microsoft® certified partner and a premiere Microsoft® Office Project training partner. We are also privileged to be a FranklinCovey alliance partner providing project management training to their clients, as well as a MindJet and Keystone Learning, LLC partner. We're established in Petaluma, California but have offices across North America. We provide project management training and consulting to a variety of clients ranging from the U.S. Marines to Dannon Yogurt, as you see in my partial client list.

The Project Management Practice, Inc. (PM Practice) began with one mission – bringing project management to the real world. For further information: www.pmpractice.com

Why Another Project Management Book?

I reach out to thousands of people annually through consulting, instructor led training, and webcasts. This book is one more medium I can use to share my experiences and help others successfully manage their projects.

Some authors need to undertake extensive research and conduct numerous interviews to develop the models, material, and cases for their books. Alternatively, 25 years in management and consulting has exposed me to a wealth of information and resources that I draw upon and summarize in this book. I have been able to see and discuss the "dirty laundry", as well as experience what happens behind the scenes in project management across a wide variety products, industries, and associations which have ranged from the American Quarter Horse Association to the Canadian Chinese Business Development Association. This experience includes products like yogurt, fiberglass, semiconductors and software, as well as industries such as casinos, banks, government, military and police, hi-tech, pulp and paper, restaurant, legal, telecommunication, pharmaceutical, transportation and oil and gas.

In addition to drawing upon my business experience, I find that when consulting and training, I can relate to individuals by bringing my personal experiences as a father and as a sports enthusiast to the table. Complementing a wealth of project management knowledge are parallels between sound project management guidelines and rules in a sport that I am passionate about – Hockey. I will use the hockey analogy throughout this book to provide the reader a unique learning dimension.

The Project Management Play Book is designed to be your guide as you enter the project management game. This book is filled with tools. At the end of the book, a summary of the tools (i.e.,

techniques, habits, and graphics) that have this indicator symbol is included.

I refer to this collection of tools as the "sports bag". These tools help you score a goal by meeting expectations and delivering on time and in budget. This book also includes a CD that encompasses a Microsoft Office PowerPoint deck that follows the book structure, and various Project Management forms.

Bottom line: this is not a textbook; it is not based on academic models. Instead, it is based on real world experience that works. The information is presented in a light and concise fashion and it recommends a similar streamlined approach to managing projects.

The Sports Bag

What is the Game Plan?

Throughout this manual, I reference the four main stages of the project management process, modified but derived, from the Project Management Institute's Project Management Body of Knowledge (PMBOK), and their respective supporting tools, as follows:

I D E A

What are the Benefits to my Organization?

This approach to project management helps Project Managers and Project Team Members create, plan, implement, and complete projects on time and within budget. The bottom-line benefits include:

- Decreased costs through better planning, less repeated work, and smarter workload management
- Better use of resources and time
- Strengthened cooperation and buy-in by team members and stakeholders
- The highest expected ROI in cost savings, customer satisfaction, increased profits and overall resource utilization productivity
- A common process and toolset across departments
- Focusing on the right project at the right time
- Earlier recognition of potential problems
- Greater control over a project's progress
- Transferring all necessary knowledge and skills to allow Project Managers and Team Leaders to better manage projects and meet stakeholder expectations

11

- Empowering Project Managers and Team Leaders to modify and use the solution to benefit their respective projects and project teams

- Automating the work breakdown structure by planning and tracking projects using a standard and reusable template, customized for the process. This consistent and easy-to-use process provides faster and more accurate project information that assists decision making with regard to trade-off between cost, schedule, and scope

- Reduced time and money spent backtracking and re-writing a plan

What are the Supporting Forms?

On the CD accompanying, and printed in the back of this book, I have provided sample project management forms. These forms can be used throughout the project lifecycle to create important project management deliverables such as: Project Scope Document, Project Communication Plan, Risk Assessment, Change Request Form, Status Reports Meeting Planner, Milestone Acceptance Document, Project Evaluation Worksheet, Project Review Report and Project Acceptance Document. There is also a PowerPoint deck following *The Project Management Play Book* on the CD.

Chapter 1:
1.0 The Starting Point

Questions to Answer

1. What is a Project?

2. What Characteristics are Common to all Projects?

3. What is the Project Life Cycle?

4. What is Project Management?

5. Who is a Project Manager?

6. Why use Project Management?

7. Why do Projects Fail?

8. What are Project Management Success Factors?

9. How do we Synergize with other Project Resources?

10. Project Resources Behavior Styles – "The Birds"

What is a Project?

All projects have some common characteristics. If we examine those common characteristics, we can roll them together to become a definition of a project.

First, all projects are temporary. They do come to an end. They have a timeline. In fact, a time constraint is one of the three triple constraints, as are limited resources, such as human or financial resources and scope/quality. The scope defines the parameters of a project and lists its specific and measurable deliverables.

A project is a complex series of non-routine tasks directed to meet a specific goal.

Projects have three main characteristics:

- Temporary (all projects come to an end)
- Limited Resources
- Specific and Measurable Deliverables

Project management is not .... **Just Do It!** As you can clearly see in the following graphic, the end result of trying to get the elephant into a trailer that is too small is project failure. It's not even possible, (and due to the position of the elephant's tail in proximity to the handler, there is considerable risk!) Many projects start like this. There is no comprehension that the end result might not be technically or financially feasible, coupled with a lack of awareness of potential risks. They "Just Do It".

JUST DO IT... possibly the three most dangerous words in project management. How can three words, popularized by a Nike™ Corporation ad campaign, be so wrong for organizations wanting to implement projects? Quite simply, organizations are spending billions of dollars "just doing it" to the wrong things, at the wrong time, and in the wrong way. Project leaders dive right into implementation, disregarding or misunderstanding the whole of project management as a practice, which requires undergoing critical steps prior to execution. Sometimes, we erroneously disguise this as being entrepreneurial. Think of the story of the project leader who turns to his engineer and says, "You start development and I will go find out what the customer really wants".

Understanding that implementing effective project management requires a framework with processes, tools and skills to support it, will go a long way to ensure success. Couple that with a clearly defined mission, vision and strategy that act as the primary filter for project decision-making, organizations can move past the "just do it" approach into doing the right projects, at the right time, in the right way.

What Characteristics are Common to all Projects?

Projects have objectives. Projects have well-defined deliverables, deadlines, and budgets. You can divide the project objective into work packages and tasks. Many projects on a particular subject become a program.

Projects are temporary. You know when the project will end before it begins. A temporary team performs the tasks in a project.

Projects have a life cycle. Like organic entities, projects have life cycles: slow start, momentum and termination.

Projects have interdependencies. The project is embedded in the strategy of the organization and interacts with the ongoing operations as well as other projects.

Projects are unique. Every project has unique elements. No two projects are the same and are a vehicle of change.

Projects involve conflict. The project manager lives in a world of conflict. You must define authority figures, especially for the project. Projects compete with functional departments for personnel and facilities. Project team members have two bosses at the same time.

Projects represent change. The value of the change justifies the project. Examples of change include a new building, a new road, a new software application or an upgrade to an existing one.

What is the Project Life Cycle?

All projects have life cycles.

- Projects Begin
- Projects Have a Middle
- Projects End (Really!)

Each project management process stage represents one of the four Pillars of Project Management. Use them for early, clear and decisive Go/No Go Decision Points:

Initiate---→ Exit – Key Go/No Go Decision Point

Plan ---→ Exit – Key Go/No Go Decision Point

Project vs. Process – What is the difference?

- Processes – routine - repetitive activities
- Projects – non-routine - unique activities

What is Project Management?

In a classroom setting, I often ask the participants to identify the characteristics of an effective project manager. They indicate characteristics that you can see under the art side of this diagram.

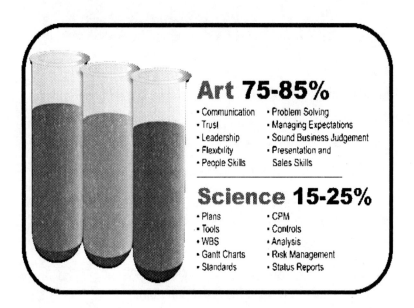

Art 75-85%

- Communication
- Trust
- Leadership
- Flexibility
- People Skills

- Problem Solving
- Managing Expectations
- Sound Business Judgement
- Presentation and
  Sales Skills

Science 15-25%

- Plans
- Tools
- WBS
- Gantt Charts
- Standards

- CPM
- Controls
- Analysis
- Risk Management
- Status Reports

When I was living in the San Francisco Bay area, I would pick up the local newspaper and look at the career ads for project managers. I found things like, "...they must have five years of C++ programming".

A person with five years of programming experience has potentially been locked in a cubicle for eight to ten hours a day, not communicating, not leading, not motivating. They then are pulled from their comfort zone to be a leader and a motivator.

This approach does not work well; in fact what happens is that the accidental project manager is created – someone who is the best technical person, but the possibly the worst manager. And the Peter Principle kicks in; people get promoted to the level of incompetency and remain there.

What is a Project Manager?

The Project Manager is the person who identifies the project's hurdles, then gets over, under, around or through them to deliver the project on time and within budget.

The **Project Manager (PM)** is the primary leader, communicator, coordinator, and champion for a project. The PM is a temporary position, selected from within the organization early in the project life cycle.

Project Managers apply the knowledge, skills, tools and techniques to project activities/tasks, in order to meet stakeholder needs and expectations.

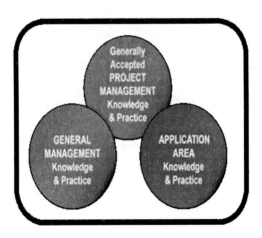

Why use Project Management?

"Actual experience with project management indicates the majority of organizations using it experience better control and better customer relations. A significant proportion of users also report shorter development times, lower costs, higher quality and reliability and higher profit margins. Other reported advantages include a sharper orientation towards results, better interdepartmental coordination and higher worker morale," says E.W. Davis, <u>CPM Use in Top 400 Construction Firms, Construction Division Journal</u>, American Society of Civil Engineers.

Some of the reasons organizations implement project management disciplines for their projects include:

- Providing clear descriptions of the work to be performed, minimizing surprises and conflicts

- Easier identification of responsibilities and assignments for specific tasks and activities

- Simplification of tracking functional responsibilities to ensure that you account for all activities, regardless of personnel turnover

- Reducing the need for continuous reporting

- Time limits for task completion are easier to specify

- Trade-off analysis for making project decisions becomes possible.

- Enabling the measurement of accomplishment against plans

- Exposing problems in advance, allowing for corrective action

- Improved estimating skills for future planning

- Objectives that cannot be met, or will be exceeded, are identified early

Why do Projects Fail?

I imagine most readers have been involved in projects that have failed or, at least, not gone so well. Over the years I've seen a number of them and let's be honest, I've probably caused one or two as well! But the bottom line is, clients are not bringing project management consultants in because, "things are going great!", "everybody's getting along with love, peace and harmony" or "the project will be delivered on-time and in budget".

Recently I worked with a client in the pulp and paper business that had spent $800,000 on a project that was basically going nowhere. They asked me to come in and conduct an analysis.

The first question I asked was, "do you have a Scope Document or maybe you call it a 'Project Charter' or Project Initiation Document or anything that defines the parameters, assumptions, specific and measurable deliverables?"

Well you can guess the response. It was, "No". .

When I asked why not, they said the project was developing an intranet application. That it was dynamic and fluid, and therefore they felt they didn't need one. I could smell the "B.S." right away.

So the next question I asked was, "Did you do a formal Risk Analysis?" They hadn't done that either, although they were using some complex technology, I found the only person who knew how to program that technology had moved to San Jose. This was certainly a foreseeable risk!

I then asked, "Do you have a Project Schedule to plan what you didn't know you were commissioned to build?" In fact, they did have one – they pulled out 18 pages from Microsoft® Project that could only be defined as garbage. There was no comprehensible work breakdown structure or any other type of work package. The resource list showed all kinds of over allocation and none of the tasks had been updated.

So, we decided to start over from the beginning and define the objectives. Once the objectives were defined in specific and measurable terms, we didn't merely create a project to achieve those objectives, we did an "As Is Analysis" to determine their current situation.

After a few site visits, the analysis showed they already had a solution that satisfied 80% of the now known objectives. I asked, "Good enough?". The client said, "Good enough!" and they pulled the plug on that bizarre project and saved $1.2 million dollars.

That's just one example of a project that wasn't going so well.

Throughout your career you have probably seen scenarios similar to this project. The following are some studies that list a few of the consequences of project failure. **Failing to Plan is Planning to Fail!** Consider This...

A Major Consulting firm's study of 300 large companies found:

- 65% of respondents reported projects:

  o Grossly over budget

  o Far behind in schedule

  o Technology not performing

  o Over 50% of executives believed this to be "normal"

An International Research firms recent survey of 175,000 IT projects, reports:

- 88% of projects run over schedule, over budget or both

- Average cost overrun: 89% of original estimate

- Average time overrun:222% of original estimate

- For every 100 projects there are 94 restarts

When Bad Things Happen to Good Projects, CIO Magazine reported:

- 40% of IT application development projects are canceled before completion

- 33% of the remaining projects are challenged by cost/time overruns or changes in scope

- Together, failed and challenged projects cost US companies and government agencies an estimated $145 billion per year

Top Reasons for Project Failure

1. Project deliverables are not known or understood in specific and measurable terms

2. Not enough detail in the project plans; the plans do not allocate sufficient time to achieve deliverables, or have an inadequate budget and poor resource estimates

3. No risk analysis

4. Scope creep

5. Lack of buy-in

Success = Met Expectations

Failure = Expectations not Met

What are Project Management Success Factors?

Project success factors include:

- Pre-defined Business Objectives and Project Deliverables were achieved and accepted by the business (i.e., the project satisfied the business need that justified the project)

- A high quality product is fully implemented and utilized

- Project delivery met or beat it's schedule and budget targets

- There are multiple winners:

  o Project participants have pride of ownership and feel good about their work

  o The customer is happy

  o Management has met its goals

- Project results helped build a good reputation

- Methods are in place for continual monitoring and evaluation

- Clear authority for the Project Manager to implement the project

- Commitment to the project management methodology

- A skilled project team is in agreement on project deliverables

- A complete project plan is understood by all participants
- Objectives that contribute to the larger goals of the organization
- Tracking and monitoring methods that allow for regular communication on status and results, minimizing the need for excessive meetings and reports

Successful projects require:

✓ Clear alignment with business goals and strategies

✓ "Project Governance" - Vocal sponsorship and active guidance from Business Owners

✓ Funding and committed resources

The Strategic Planning Pyramid illustrates the importance of connecting your projects to strategic initiatives or long-term goals and, in turn, to the mission.

For example, one of my culinary clients had a mission statement of *"Continually exceeding customer's expectations profitably"*. They had a strategic initiative to improve the customer satisfaction level from an already high 9.2 out of 10 to 9.5 out of 10.

They had three projects associated with that strategic goal, one had to do with Menu, a second had to do with Logistics and a third had to do with Entertainment.

So on a given day, when one of the project team members would be auditioning a band to entertain on the ship, they could justifiably say that the task tied to the Entertainment Project. And the Entertainment Project supported the goal of receiving a 9.5 Customer Satisfaction level and in turn, that goal supported the Mission Statement.

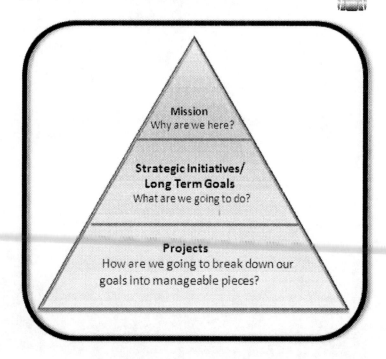

Mission
Why are we here?

Strategic Initiatives/
Long Term Goals
What are we going to do?

Projects
How are we going to break down our
goals into manageable pieces?

Success means meeting expectations. Dr. Stephen Covey, in his book, _The 7 Habits of Highly Effective People,_ identified Habit 2 as "Begin with the End in Mind".

In this diagram, you can see the customer's end in mind was simply a tire on a rope. It is not necessary to go through all these incorrect steps and associated time and costs if one spends time, upfront, understanding the expectations and then drives toward them to meet success.

How do we Synergize with Other Project Resources?

Project Mapping is a way to practice Habit 6, to _"Synergize"_ from _The 7 Habits of Highly Effective People_. It's a fast, random and colorful way of brainstorming with all participants.

As you know, a key rule of brainstorming is there are no wrong answers. You may already be familiar with this technique and may know it as Thought Mapping, Mind Mapping or even the Fish Bone Technique.

The overall idea is to put the central thought in the middle circle, be it Risks or the Project Work Breakdown Structure (WBS), Change Control Methods or the Project. In turn, make main branches on the outside to a level of detail as appropriate.

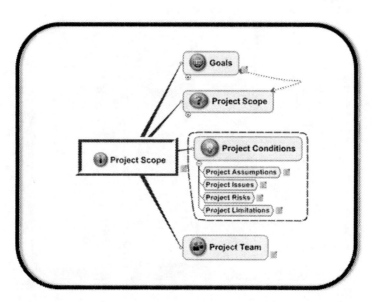

I have used this technique numerous times, particularly with clients that need a facilitator to obtain the next level of collaboration and communication within their groups.

Working with a Military client, we had a project that involved enlisted men, officers, and civilians, both union and management. It was necessary to get everyone's co-operation. We decided to segment people into four different groups and had them brainstorm components of the project, and in turn we brought all those pieces together.

In a short one-day session, we were able to walk out with a clear scope, detailed 600 line Microsoft® Office Project plan and a completed Risk Analysis. Furthermore, we had agreement and collaboration amongst all the diverse parties.

Often in teaching Microsoft® Office Project, I tell people that they can be a 'guru' in Microsoft® Office Project and know how to make it sing and dance, but if they close their door and build schedules in isolation, they will not get stakeholder buy-in. The lack of buy-in is one of the top reasons why projects fail.

The key is to: synergize with the participants to build a plan

And then: present a draft to them so they can kick some holes in it

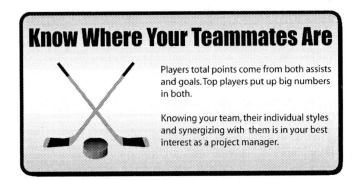

Know Where Your Teammates Are

Players total points come from both assists and goals. Top players put up big numbers in both.

Knowing your team, their individual styles and synergizing with them is in your best interest as a project manager.

Project Resources Behavior Styles – "The Birds"

Individual project resources are going to approach and handle problems in different ways. They may be more right-brain dominant; creative, artistic, and spatial. More often than not, you'll find people in marketing, sales, and training departments being right-brain dominant. Alternatively, perhaps the IT department employees may be more left-brain dominant; more linear, mathematical, technical, and logical. Despite how they approach things, we need to understand their perspectives and be able to extract the required information. Furthermore, understanding different perspectives helps project managers maximize the information from project stakeholders and minimize conflict between project resources coming from opposite styles.

The following example goes beyond a right brain, left brain perspective, and defines four different quadrants with their respective high level characteristics.

This is a simple example, based on two key questions.

The first question on the Y axis rates a person's expressiveness 0, being very shy and very quiet, to 10 being the life of the party.

The X axis rates a person's assertiveness, 0 being a person who hangs back, asks questions, and tests the water before jumping. A 10 rating would be someone who is quite assertive, who would tend to tell more than they ask.

Based on answering these questions on a scale of 0 to 10, a person's high level characteristics are matched in one of these four quadrants. Each quadrant reflects a Bird, in lieu of a psychology term or name, and defines: what motivates them, what they do not like which is indicated in the diagram with a circle and line through it, and the questions they will most likely be concerned about regarding your project.

End of Getting Started

Now let's Start Discovering and Applying
Project Management Tools through the
Project Life Cycle

Chapter 2:
2.0 Project Initiation

Questions to Answer

1. Who are the Project Stakeholders?
2. What are their Expectations?
3. How do we Document the Project Scope?

Project Initiation Introduction

Project Initiation is about visualizing your end result before you begin. In fact, that relates directly to Habit 2 in The 7 Habits of Highly Effective People, "Begin with the End in Mind". The output of the initiation stage is a Scope Document that has three 'C's. It's Clear, Concise and Consistent.

In order to develop the Scope Document, we need to understand: who are the project stakeholders, what are their expectations, and then document the overall scope.

Who are the Project Stakeholders?

The **Project Stakeholders** are those parties impacted by the project and have an interest in its outcome. They may include the people who establish project deliverables and constraints, and implement the strategies and schedules. Examples of project stakeholders include project sponsors, project managers, line managers, team members, customers (internal and external), outside agencies and vendors.

It can sometimes be an overwhelming challenge for a project manager to juggle all of the stakeholders. It can also result in a lot of frustration if one does not identify the key project stakeholders upfront. The lack of identifying them in the initiation stage will probably result in them identifying themselves during the execution stage and could result in changing the overall direction of the project.

So, it's important to understand whose expectations we should be meeting and to identify not just one of them, but to ensure all the key stakeholders have been properly identified.

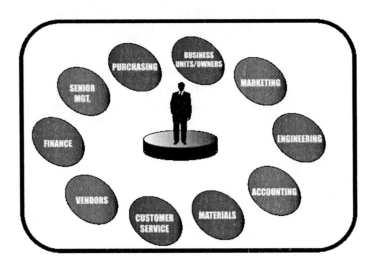

In working with a major association, I was called to determine a problem with the system they'd implemented. I found the system was highly customizable but the project manager had not identified all of the key stakeholders. He had only identified one of the four. And in turn, had built and implemented the system to satisfy only that key stakeholder's overall needs.

The other three (or 75%) directors weren't at all satisfied with the solution. They thought it was a technology problem. We quickly communicated it wasn't a technology problem – it was a problem with the project manager not being able to identify all the key stakeholders; therefore he didn't define all of the requirements and of course, the system wasn't meeting the requirements of all key stakeholders.

Over the years, I have developed an acronym to help us identify key stakeholders. I've defined those as

- the people with the **M**oney – sometimes this is the people with the money or the budget-holder;
- the people with the **A**uthority to deploy the resources or the authority to say yes or no;
- a party that represents the end-user or the person who's going to **N**eed the product or service that is being implemented.

So, we're looking for the **MAN**, but we also don't want to forget we need to identify key stakeholders who have the **W**illingness and **O**ptimism to work with us in a spirit of co-operation. So the real project key stakeholders are defined as the W.O.M.A.N..

The key project stakeholders are those that can say 'Yes' or 'No' to the project and will determine its success factors. They have the**:**

W Willingness

O Optimism

M Money / Means

A Authority

N Need

What are Their Expectations?

Good project planning requires asking and answering several questions in order to begin the process. We have developed the following techniques to facilitate the questioning process:

- Begin with the end in mind

    o Identify all stakeholders

    o Interview key stakeholders and determine:

      - Their vision of the end results
      - The prioritized deliverables

Needs Assessment

- Needs exist on a variety of levels
- Needs should be prioritized and separated from wants
- Projects often have conflicting needs
- Clients often do not actually know, or understand, their needs

Very often, there is a limited time to perform a needs analysis. Therefore, it is essential that you have a framework for structuring your questions and collecting information. The following baseball example is an excellent framework.

For many years, I have used this baseball framework as a method for gathering requirements and understanding a client's current situation, future needs and existing problems.

Recently, I was asked to do a diagnosis of project management processes and solutions that were being employed by a company involved in the software development for healthcare insurance.

Going to 'First Base', I interviewed 18 people about the **current situation**. I discovered they basically had a few forms that they filled out. They closed projects when the customer stopped calling.

Well, I moved forward to 'Second Base' to discuss **future needs**.

Their response, "... we've bought 300 licenses of Microsoft Project®. We'd like to know how to use it. We'd like to know how to do a risk analysis, to have clear, concise and consistent scope documents and to manage change".

I then moved to 'Third Base', because even as a hockey player I learned that you can't run to home plate from second base and score a run, if you skip third base.

From my third base perspective I asked, "What kind of **existing problems** are you facing?" And they indicated that they were hit during their last quarter with $500,000 in penalties for late implementations. They also estimated they left approximately $750,000 of billable work on the table. In other words, they had a customer calling and requesting a change. They couldn't really prove to the customer it was a change in scope because they didn't have a scope document. They were feeling guilty because, well, they were running late; therefore, they would say yes.

But in hindsight they felt the customer request was beyond scope. If they could have proved it, they would have billed for the extra requested work, which they did not, and subsequently lost the estimated $750,000 in revenue. We reviewed this difficult lesson learned. We executed a staged-in solution which involved proactively solving these problems, while satisfying their specific and measurable needs.

By playing baseball, we've practiced Habit 5 of The 7 Habits of Highly Effective People where we "Seek First to Understand' – understand things like current situation, future needs and existing problems, before "Being Understood" and phasing in our solution.

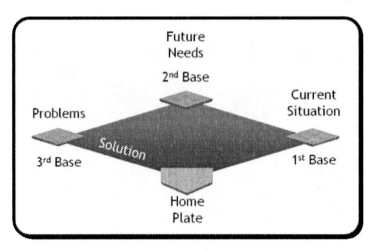

Core Question for Key Stakeholders:

"As you think about your project's successful outcomes what is important to you?"

More Questions:

1st Base Question: Where are you now with _____?

2nd Base Question: Where do you want to be?

3rd Base Question: What are the problems with the current situation?

Let's Have a Feast

Avoid using poorly defined, ambiguous terms, such as Effective, Efficient, Better, Faster, Improved, Profitable, and More.

It's as if I was saying, "Let's have a feast". Some people may be envisioning this feast as going to a fast-food restaurant, having french-fries, burgers and a Cola. Others may envision the feast as going to a fine-dining restaurant, sitting down with white linens, having some drinks, an appetizer, a salad, soup du jour, a sorbet and an entree with Chardonnay and finishing with Crème Brule.

The number one reason why projects fail are the lack of specific and measurable deliverables. I imagine a majority of you have heard things like, "Make it better!" "Faster!" "Improve!" "Portable" "Scalable" "Profitable" and the inevitable "User Friendly" scope instruction.

What do they mean? They mean absolutely nothing!

When we use ambiguously-defined words like "feast" or "faster," different people hear the same word and may have very different perceptions in defining the project scope.

So instead, what you want to do is ensure your deliverables are not dumb, but are SMART!

Ensure your scope statement is S.M.A.R.T.

Specific

Measurable

Achievable

Relevant

Time Constrained

Ask the Right Questions

A CEO of a major consulting firm once wanted to determine the difference between the good and the great project managers they employed. They did a three month study, in which a team of consultants observed the project managers, documenting their findings and determining the delta between the good and the great.

When they reported the findings to the CEO, they found the most observable difference was that great project managers asked more questions.

Asking more questions is a start, but if you're running around the bases and all you're hearing are, "yes", "no" and "I don't know" responses, perhaps you're not asking the right types of questions.

You may want to incorporate three types of questions illustrated in the Questioning Funnel and Scale Diagrams below:

- **Open-ended Questions-** the five "w's" (who, what, when, where, why) plus "how" and reflective questions.

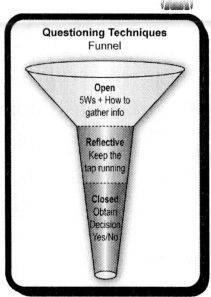

- **Reflective Questions-** keep the tap running, things like, "Oh, really?" – parroting back what you've heard; or, "That's interesting", or "Tell me more". Or, one we're famous for in Canada is, "Eh?"

- **Closed Questions-** when you're merely looking for a decision – "Was the budget $500,000?" "Yes." "Done!" a closed-ended question will worked well.

However, if all you have in your arsenal are closed-ended questions, you'll have a short information-gathering time and you probably will not understand the complete expectations.

As a guideline, there's a recommended balance between open (30%), reflective (60%) and closed-ended (10%) questions.

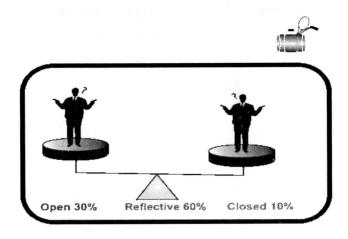

Open 30%   Reflective 60%   Closed 10%

To ensure you maximize information obtained from your stakeholders, make sure you utilize a balance of questioning techniques, as illustrated in the Funnel and Scale diagrams.

How do we Document the Project Scope?

A project scope statement document for your project must be in harmony with the overall expectations of your key stakeholders to obtain buy-in. It is a written document that forms the basis for an agreement between the project team and the project customer.

What is not on paper has not been said!

The Scope Document concisely and clearly identifies the:

- What?
- When?
- Where?
- How Much?
- Why = The fit with a Strategic Initiative
- Assumptions

The scope statement consists of two separate sections:

1. Project Description: a few brief and concise sentences

   - Not a requirements document or spec sheet
   - Identifies Key constraints and supporting statements

2. Expected Outcomes / Success Criteria:

   - Expected Results *(In terms of SMART Outcomes - Accomplishments)*

When developing a Scope Statement:

Develop a Scope Statement in a group setting using a brainstorming technique such as Project Mapping mentioned earlier. This technique generates discussion on objectives, constraints, assumptions, and lessons learned from previous projects, which add significant value to the vision / scope statement.

- Review stakeholder interview results
- Record ideas from the group, on the project's what, when, and where
- Record ideas from the group on desired results and expected outcomes
- Translate these ideas into more of a narrative format for a first draft
- Stay flexible. Use people-to-people contact and stress fast response both ways
- Insist on top management participation. They can make or break a project, and may be the most important variable
- Beware of future spending plans. This may eliminate the tendency to underestimate
- Test assumptions. Remember that most professionals are too optimistic

- Review the draft document with all stakeholders. While reviewing the draft, record any comments related to the scope regarding risks, assumptions, definitions, issues, opportunities, constraints, and strategies. During the review, apply the SMART checklist to ensure all stakeholders begin with the end in mind

- Integrate the feedback into a final draft

- Complete the Scope Statement form (see Project Plan Template)

Stay Onside!

In hockey the puck must enter the offensive zone ahead of the attacking player.

Not listening in project management or getting ahead of your key stakeholders by making assumptions will result in not meeting expectations.

End of Initiation

Formally recognize that a new project exists or that an existing project should continue.

"Get out while the Getting is Good"

"Exit Early and Save Significant Time and Money!"

Chapter 3:

3.0 Project Design (Planning)

Questions to Answer

1. What are the Project Scheduling/Planning Steps?
2. How do we Plan Procurement?
3. How do we Plan for Quality?

"A failure to plan, is planning to fail"

Plan/Design Introduction

Planning is the process of out-guessing / out-smarting failure. The deliverables in this section are a Risk Analysis, Detailed Project Schedule, Procurement Plan, and Quality Plan. In order to build these, we need to answer these questions:

- Where do we start?
- What are the steps in putting together the project plan?
- How do we identify and schedule parts of the plan?
- How do we identify the required resources?

Not necessarily the easiest questions to answer!

So often people say, "Forget about it!" "I don't have time to plan. Let's just do it! But we all know a failure to plan, is planning to fail.

Typical complaints about planning

- "I do not have time to plan"
- "I would not know where to begin"
- "You know management wants results, not plans"
- "I know the theory, but around here I never get a chance to exercise it"

Unfortunately, these typical complaints also result in the typical project steps. As they go through the cycle, a new project comes up to which management says, "We are very enthusiastic about it" and repeats the following typical seven steps in ascending order.

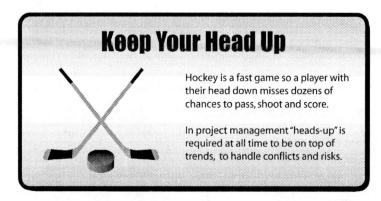

Keep Your Head Up

Hockey is a fast game so a player with their head down misses dozens of chances to pass, shoot and score.

In project management "heads-up" is required at all time to be on top of trends, to handle conflicts and risks.

Typical Project Steps

1. Unwarranted enthusiasm
2. Uncritical acceptance
3. Growing concern
4. Unmitigated disaster
5. Search for the guilty
6. Punish the innocent
7. Promote the uninvolved

Remember the Return on Investment

For every moment you spend doing effective planning, you will obtain five moments saved during execution.

After you realize the benefit of planning there is no going back!

What Are the Project Scheduling Steps?

1. Review Scope Statement
2. Determine Dominating Factors – Triple Constraint

3. Define and Quantify Risks
4. Develop the Work Breakdown Structure

    a. Determine Work Packages / Activities

    b. Determine Project Tasks

    c. Set the Milestones

5. Determine the Task Duration
6. Sequence the Activities for Efficiency and Logical Connections
7. Identify the Critical Path
8. List the Project Resources
9. Assign Resources to Tasks
10. Optimize the Plan
11. Produce Reports and Communicate the Plan
12. Review the Feasibility of the Project (time, cost, scope, quality, risks)
13. Document Assumptions and Issues (ongoing process throughout the project)
14. Obtain Approval of the Plan
15. Freeze the Plan (set the baseline)

Step 1 – Review Scope Statement

The Scope Statement is the project's main target. It is the glue between the project team and the key stakeholders. It also dictates the development of the Work Breakdown Structure (WBS), as well as provides an opportunity to identify project risks. Review the Scope Statement with the Project Sponsor, Key Stakeholders, and Project Team Members as the team develops.

Remember not to be defensive when reviewing the Scope Statement; be accepting of necessary input and feedback. Incorporate the feedback from key stakeholders and team members to create buy in at all levels of the project. Be very cautious of ambiguous words and try to seek clarity on all words in the scope statement. During discussions around the Scope Statement, be sure the following have been captured; assumptions, SMART deliverables, clarifications, and constraints.

Step 2 - Project Management Driving Forces

The definition of project objectives is making the deliverables within a certain period, with a given budget. The three driving forces influencing projects are:

- The deadline: Time
- Budget restrictions: Money, Resources
- Scope or Quality

What is Your Priority?

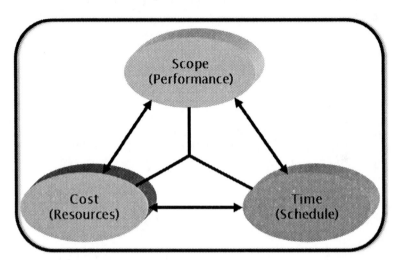

The bottom line is, "Do you want it fast, good or cheap? Pick two." You can guess on the prioritization of these constraints, though you'll have a one in three chance of guessing right. Working with clients, I can think of numerous times based on the feedback I was given at that point, I would have guessed wrong.

One client was talking extensively about the comprehension technology and wanted a business plan built. I thought scope was the most important factor.   When asked about the prioritization of the constraints, he indicated to me the plan had to be done in 20 days, as it needed to be presented at their Annual Meeting, which was already scheduled. As a result of the discussion you can imagine the scope was diminished quickly.

The Triple Constraint is one of the core models of project management. We will be revisiting the Triple Constraint as we quantify risks and again as we attempt to optimize the schedule.

Project Managers must discover which force is dominant. Knowing this and scheduling accordingly is vital to the success of the project. Depending on which driving force is dominant, the same project will result in three very different schedules. All project managers should continuously ask which factor is most, and which is least important, throughout the course of the project.

Step 3 – Define and Quantify Risks

Failing to recognize the issues that create the most risk for a project will result in project failure. Projects can be at risk for many reasons: high cost, failure to give a good return on investment, the use of new technologies, or poor definition of objectives by the client.

The Project Manager's challenge is to identify the variables which may cause the project to fail. By recognizing which variables are creating the risk, the project manager plans for ways to limit that risk.

For example, if you were planning a picnic in the greater Seattle area, one of the risks would of course be rain. Then, you need to look at the probability of rain. I live not too far from Seattle, and I suggest the probability is 100% that it will rain!

The impact of 200 people standing out there – cold, wet and miserable, is pretty high on the impact scale.

Next thing we'll need is a solution. Let's plan to have tents available and in the event it rains, everyone can take a few steps to the right or left and enter the tents. The event will still be successful.

Lastly, we need to determine a specific resource that will be responsible for managing this risk. Not a department name, not a title, but an actual, individual name – John Smith, Jane Doe, etc.

There are a number of variables that can affect the risks within a project such as:

Size: Number of people, length of project, number of departments

Technology: Use of new software, hardware, and languages

Structure: How well are the system requirements defined

Risk increases significantly when projects begin using technology the project team is unfamiliar with. You can avoid failure if the people in charge of the project recognize the risks and plan how to manage those risks. The following steps are outlined to help manage risks;

1. **Identify risks.** Brainstorm the anticipated risks by identifying an event and not the outcome. For example, poor documentation is an event or factor (risk) and the outcome could be that rework is necessary and the schedule is delayed (outcome). During the brainstorming session, when an outcome is identified, ask what could cause the outcome and the risk will be the answer to the question.

Examples of typical events or risks in an IT project include:

- Lack of resource participation in project planning
- Server goes down
- Limited access to required equipment
- Missing resources
- Missing test plans and scenarios
- Collaboration tools not functioning
- Missing support resources
- Limited access to key stakeholders
- Insufficient resource skill levels
- Poor tools utilization by team members
- Lack of senior management support
- No documentation
- Bleeding-edge technology

2. **Assign an impact value.** Use a scale of 1 to 5 (where 1 is Low and 5 is High) to assess the impact the risk will have on the project should it occur. High risk impact represents project failure, and low impact represents minimal disruption.

   Impact

   1. Minor adjustments
   2. Impacts lowest priority performance factor
   3. Impacts medium priority performance factor
   4. Impacts highest priority performance factor
   5. Show stopper

3. **Assign a probability value.** Use a scale of 0% to 100% to assess the probability of the risk occurring. High probability represents most likely and low represents unlikely.

   Probability

   1 to 25% Low

   25% to 75% Medium

   75% to 99% High

4. **Quantify each risk.** Multiply the impact value with the probability value to assign a quantification value. For example: Impact of 4 with Probability of 75% = 300

5. **Prioritize the risks.** Reorganize the list of risks from high to low to focus the team on the risks with the greatest impact and probability. Risks with a High / High value are the highest priority. Those with a Low / Low value are the lowest priority.

6. **Determine risk response.** Brainstorm possible responses to the highest priority risks and assign actions depending on the time allocated for managing risks. Risks can be categorized as follows:

   - **Accept** – accept the consequences should they occur

   - **Mitigate** – take action to control the risk by developing contingency plans

   - **Transfer** – share the risk with others by subcontracting, purchasing insurance, etc.

7. **Assign an individual** to be responsible for tracking, reporting, and managing the risk; especially, those with a high quantification value.

8. Review the **Project Risk Plan** with the appropriate project stakeholders.

After you have brainstormed all the risks and determined the impact, probability, contingency plan and person responsible, it's easy to take the risk you've identified and in turn, populate them in a risk analysis or risk assessment form as illustrated.

Risk	Impact	Probability	Weight	Avoidance/ Contingency	Resource
	1-5	%			Responsible

I've had numerous clients say to me, "No, my boss doesn't want to see risks and problems." Risks with solutions, and risks that you have properly anticipated in order to then go over, under, around or through them to deliver your project on-time and in budget, will be appreciated.

An international research firm did a study and found that 90% of risks were foreseeable. So you need to practice Habit 1, "Be Proactive", of The 7 Habits of Highly Effective People and pro-actively anticipate the risks and develop a good workaround or backup plan.

As you can see in the following diagram, it is only those risks having high impact and high probability that you really need to pay attention to.

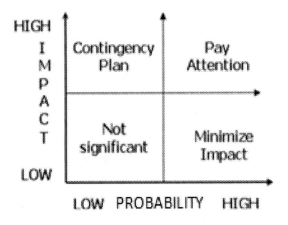

Keep Your Stick on the Ice

The blade of the hockey stick needs to be on the ice to receive, handle and shoot the puck.

Keeping your stick on the ice in Project Management means being proactive through developing a scope document, planning for risks and developing a detailed project schedule.

Step 4 - Develop the Work Breakdown Structure

A **Work Breakdown Structure (WBS)** is a hierarchical organization of the work necessary to complete the project. A WBS consists of work packages, tasks, milestones, and deliverables. It is the foundation for building a new project schedule.

There are numerous ways to break your project schedule down, such as: by deliverables, by methodology, geographical location, or module. There's no one right answer.

The key though, is to break it down to enough level of detail where you are confident in the estimates of time and budget that roll out of the project schedule.

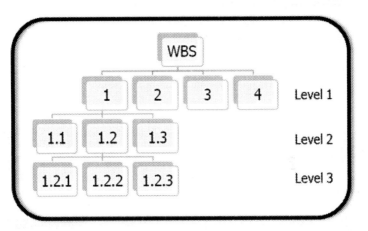

WBS Styles:

- Deliverables Based (Product / Service) Work Packages
- Functional Groups
- Geographical
- Time Phased
- Mixed

Gantt Chart Example of Time-Phased WBS

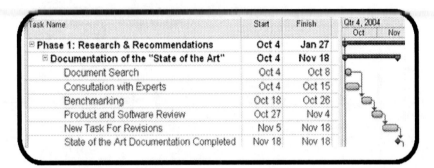

Task Name	Start	Finish	Qtr 4, 2004 Oct	Nov
⊟ Phase 1: Research & Recommendations	Oct 4	Jan 27		
⊟ Documentation of the "State of the Art"	Oct 4	Nov 18		
Document Search	Oct 4	Oct 8		
Consultation with Experts	Oct 4	Oct 15		
Benchmarking	Oct 18	Oct 26		
Product and Software Review	Oct 27	Nov 4		
New Task For Revisions	Nov 5	Nov 18		
State of the Art Documentation Completed	Nov 18	Nov 18		

Project Map Example of Phased WBS

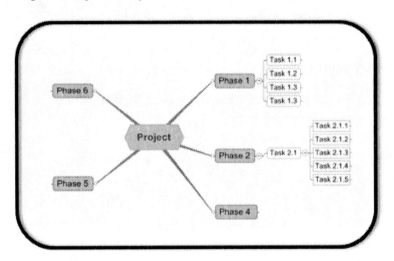

WBS Development Steps

List the Work Packages

Identify the detailed-level tasks for each work package. Categorize each detailed-level task according to the project life cycle stages. The tasks categorized in the initial stage of a project should be more precisely defined than tasks categorized in the later stages. As a stage gate approaches, the next stage tasks should be more defined and approved by the project sponsor.

- Be as precise as possible in defining the work associated with a task.

- Avoid, if possible, the combining of unrelated effort into a single task.

Determine the Project Tasks

Schedules consist of tasks and their relationship(s). A task is a work activity or event that has a defined start, a defined end and/or duration, and produces a measurable result or end product.

Defining Milestones

Milestones are important events or dates in a project, but are not tasks with work associated with them. The definition of a milestone is a task with zero duration.

Step 5 - Detemine the Task Duration

The Art of Estimating

Life would be much easier for Project Managers if computer scientists and systems professionals had designed a full proof way to estimate systems. There are many different models and methods for estimating, but none are entirely accurate. The chief reason for this is that projects and people vary greatly. Even though a project may look like another one that you have previously done, there may be great differences in organizational culture, technology, or user needs. In order to prepare an estimate for a project there are elements you must understand. These include:

- Size
- Complexity
- Risk
- Experience

Estimating Methods

There are many different models for estimating systems. We will focus on just four, yet others are available. The method a person uses depends on many things, including: previous experience, which methods the organization has used before, and which ones worked.

Choosing an Estimating Technique

Technique	Best Application
Based on Similar Project	When a previous successful plan is available with a high degree of similarity to the current project.
Standardized Task Units	When repetitive tasks are duplicated in many similar projects, requiring tasks with a history of consistent execution over a substantial time period.
Team Estimating	Always advisable when multiple people are involved; mandatory if people have special or unique expertise.
Expert Assistance	If the project is extremely costly and time critical and requires a high degree of reliability to succeed.

Step 6 - Sequence the Activities

There are three main types of dependencies – sequential, partial and concurrent. You need to link your tasks together in order to move to Step 7 and calculate the critical path.

Task Dependencies - Sequential Tasks

Sequential tasks follow in strict sequence. Task #2 cannot start until Task #1 is completed.

Sequential tasks are normally forced on the project because one task cannot start before another task is 100% completed.

- Task #1 is a predecessor of Task #2.
- Task #3 is a successor of Task #2.

Concurrent Tasks

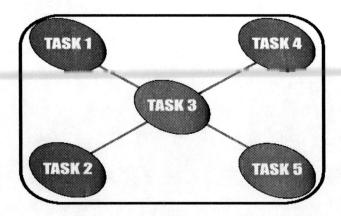

With concurrent tasks, one task requires the completion of two (or more) other tasks before it can begin. Multiple tasks can only start after the completion of a task(s).

- Task #3 cannot begin until both Task #1 and Task #2 end

- When Task #3 ends, both Task #4 and #5 can start concurrently

Multiple relationships can occur because of Go / No Go points. Task 3 has **successor** Tasks #4 and #5. Tasks #1 and #2 are **predecessors** of Task #3.

Partially Dependent Tasks

Tasks can be partially dependent. (Task #2 cannot start until Task #1 is halfway completed, and Task #3 cannot start until Task #2 is three quarters complete).

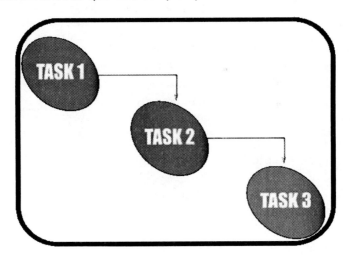

Step 7 - Identify the Critical Path

Most everyone has heard the term, Critical Path. Although when I ask people what it means, there's only a small percentage that can actually identify it correctly.

People seem to think it means any task that is important. It does not.

It's those tasks which will affect the overall end date. In any single-project network, one sequence of tasks fixes the duration of the project. Any slippage or failure to begin a task on time or a task taking longer than estimated will cause the project to finish later than planned. This sequence or path of sequentially linked tasks is the **critical path.**

A good example is preparing a Thanksgiving dinner. Since cooking the turkey takes the most time, the task of cooking the turkey is on the critical path. Cooking the potatoes takes about one hour, cooking the vegetables about a half-hour, but if you've got a 20 pound bird, cooking the turkey will take four hours in a standard oven. Therefore, tasks related to preparing the turkey are more critical or time sensitive than tasks related to preparing the potatoes or the vegetables. Other task tha may end up on the critical path may include buying and defrosting the turkey.

I've used this analogy numerous times although I should mention, it hasn't always gone over that well. I teach frequently in Europe. When I talk about preparing a Thanksgiving dinner, they, of course, look at me with quizzical frowns of concern, as they don't celebrate Thanksgiving in Europe.

Also, in the great state of Texas where I work very frequently, my good friends, told me, "Well, we don't cook our turkeys in four hours." They're often deep-fried. Frying at 3 minutes a pound, the turkey is done quicker than conventional cooking.

I've actually had a chance to deep-fry turkeys in Texas, and contrary to first impression, they're very moist and taste very good. But good for you? That's another story!

The critical path task are is the ones in which:

- The earliest and latest starts for tasks are the same
- The earliest and latest finishes for tasks are the same

The earliest start of any task is the duration of all related preceding tasks: they must be completed tasks. Earliest finish of any task is earliest start plus the **duration** of the task.

The latest finish of any task is the duration of all related succeeding tasks: they cannot commence until this task is complete. The latest start of any task is it's latest finish minus the **duration** of the task.

Tasks, which are not on the critical path, have **float time,** flexible time in a schedule where tasks can slip without causing schedule delays. The latest start minus the earliest start is the amount of float or total slack. Free float is the amount of time you can delay a task before it affects the start of any successor.

Task	Dur.	Early Start	Late Start	Early Finish	Late Finish	Float
#7	5	10	15	15	20	5
#8	10	10	10	20	20	0

Consider Task #7 in this simplified example:

> The earliest start day: 10
>
> Task #7 duration is 5 days (DUR = 5 days)
>
> Task #8 duration is 10 days (DUR = 10 days)
>
> Task #7 then has a late finish of day 20 and a late start of 15

If Task #7 starts on day 10, it will be completed at early finish at day 15.

The float for Task #7 is 15-10=5 before it would affect the project end.

Float vs. Contingency

- **Float** is the latest start subtracted from the earliest start

- **Contingency** is approved budget in reserve to cover some risks

Step 8 - List the Project Resources

Very often the project manager doesn't have a choice regarding the resources to be allocated to their project.

As a project manager, I was asked to find out why a company couldn't pay their suppliers on time and in budget. I had a highly-vested interest because, as a consultant, I was also a supplier.

They said to me, "you need to pick your team from the surplus list". That wasn't a good sign. This was a group of people who should have all been fired 10 years ago. It was very difficult to work with this team. I approached the client and said "you want me to win the game, but I only have injured players", and requested a new team.

Choosing the Right People

Skate Hard & Take Breaks Often!

Line changes happen frequently allowing players to work hard and rest on the bench before they do it again.

As a project manager you have to work hard and be aware of your resources availability and bandwidth.

Questions to ask:

- What skills are required to complete the tasks on the project?

- Where will the people come from to complete the tasks?

- How should you organize the people working on the project?

- What are the specific technical skills required to complete a task?

- How much experience should the person (people) have, in order to complete this task?

- Does a person need to have specific experience performing a task, or is general experience applicable? If so, what general experience is required?

- In addition to technical skills, what are the specific interpersonal skills required to complete this task effectively, such as good written or verbal communication skills, diplomacy, negotiating skills, or management ability?

In turn, develop a project resource pool, which includes the following information about each resource: Name, ID, Position, Department, Availability, Cost Rate, and Vacation Schedule.

Step 9 - Assigning Resources / Costs

Assigning additional resources to fixed duration tasks **will not reduce** a task's completion time. Alternatively, assigning additional resources to an effort-driven task **will reduce** the duration.

A task's cost is a function of:

Resources * Resource Rate * Percent Resource is assigned + Additional costs

Project Costs

Labor costs are the salaries and sometimes benefits paid to people who work on your project.

Material and supply costs are the costs of purchasing additional supplies and minor equipment for your project.

Vendor costs are the costs of using consultants, outside companies, or service providers to complete work on a project.

Fixed costs are costs that are unaffected by the volume of work being performed.

Allocated costs are charges assigned to a project by the company, usually as a percentage of operational overhead. Direct costs are a direct result of work, services, or materials used on a project.

Variable costs are costs that change with time or volume.

Capital expenditures are purchases of large, permanent machines, facilities, or equipment.

Step 10 - Optimize the Plan

At this point, the project schedule is built. There are work packages, stages, tasks, milestones, duration estimates, dependencies, and relationships between tasks. A critical path has been calculated, resources defined and resources allocated. And inevitably you can now determine the total cost, total work and total time for your project.

Odds are high those metrics are not in line with the desired time, desired dollars or desired work. You'll need to optimize the plan. But what do you do first? Well, that's based again on the prioritization of the triple constraints.

If scope has the greatest degree of flexibility, then start pulling things out of the Work Breakdown Structure. If resources or dollars have the greatest degree of flexibility, perhaps adding more resources will get things done faster. If time has the greatest degree of flexibility, perhaps letting the project slip, or schedules slide until resources are available at the optimal rate might be the right thing to do.

The combination of directing these three things will help build the optimal schedule.

Final Schedule Check List

Assumptions	No assumptions are violated
Critical Path	Clearly marked on the network diagram
Consensus	All major participants have reviewed dates for completeness and accuracy
Dates	All holidays and special events have been noted appropriately; no resource Conflicts exist
Chart	Clearly specifies tasks, durations, individual responsibilities, and target start and finish dates
Float	The plan contains adequate float and contingency

Resource Conflicts

Resource conflicts exist when a resource must do more than one thing at the same time, thus exceeding the resource's availability.

To resolve conflicts:

- Allocate alternative resources

- Review overtime

- Extend working times, split tasks up into smaller chunks

- Reschedule with less busy time frames or resources

- Change task relationships

- Consider alternative methodologies

- Eliminate tasks

- Reallocate resources

- Increase the number of available hours in a day or week

- Postpone vacations

Reducing Project Costs

- Allocate alternative (less expensive) resources

- Reduce duration

- Change methodologies

- Eliminate scope

Step 11 - Produce Reports

Project Management Reports

"A picture is worth a thousand words." And as one of Billy Crystal's characters explained "It's better to look good than be good". While these statements may or may not exactly apply to project management, the fact remains Project Managers generally compete for scarce resources. Sales skills are important, and reports are your sales tools.

Gantt Charts

Designed by Henry Gantt in early 1900, the Gantt chart is a horizontal graphic that illustrates the relationship between task and time. Gantt charts show summary and detail tasks.

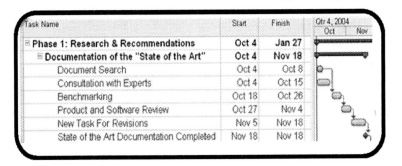

Task Name	Start	Finish	Qtr 4, 2004	
			Oct	Nov
⊟ Phase 1: Research & Recommendations	Oct 4	Jan 27		
⊟ Documentation of the "State of the Art"	Oct 4	Nov 18		
Document Search	Oct 4	Oct 8		
Consultation with Experts	Oct 4	Oct 15		
Benchmarking	Oct 18	Oct 26		
Product and Software Review	Oct 27	Nov 4		
New Task For Revisions	Nov 5	Nov 18		
State of the Art Documentation Completed	Nov 18	Nov 18		

Precedence or Network Diagram Charts

Precedence or Network Diagramming charts clearly represent the dependencies between tasks. Information in each node can include as little as the WBS code or as much as task name, start, and end dates, etc.

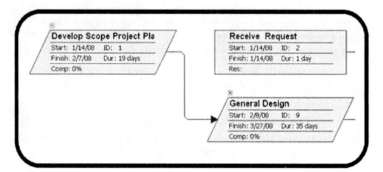

Calendar Report shows detailed tasks on a calendar

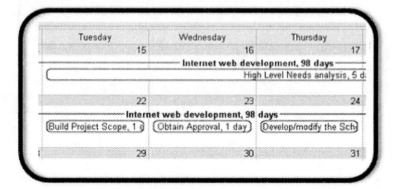

Resource Reports provides resource allocation data

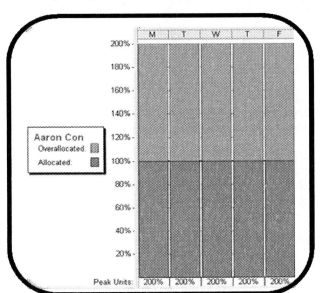

Step 12 - Establishing a Project's Feasibility

Key questions to ask when determining a project's feasibility include:

- Does the project fit into the overall goals and objectives of the organization, as established by executive management?
- Does the project fit into the cultural framework of the organization?
- Are the potential benefits of completing the project worth the resources required to implement it?
- Are the right resources available?
- Do we have someone with career project experience (CPE) to lead the project team?
- Is enough time available to complete the project?
- Will enough money be available to implement the project with the appropriate level of quality?
- Is the timing for this project appropriate? Will the project be cost effective or profitable?

Step 13 - Document Key Project Issues and Assumptions

- Are the resources qualified for this project?
- Is there a due date when the project must absolutely be complete?
- Is overtime allowed?
- Are there any holidays or other breaks during this project?
- Does the project have approval for additional resources and people?
- Have you documented the work schedules and availability of all resources?
- Are there internal politics involved?
- Have you identified all predecessors?
- Are resources located locally or globally?

Step 14 - Obtain Approval

As you have obtained input from all stakeholders and team members throughout the planning process, approval should be possible. Keep in mind, it may be necessary to develop an initial project plan and then develop several iterations afterwards.

Step 15 - Freeze the Plan

After the plan is approved, set a baseline or freeze the plan. This is essential in order to effectively track actuals to the plan and measure variance. It is this variance that enables informed decision making during the execution of the project.

How do we Plan Procurement?

Over the years I've worked with many materials management departments who can add considerable value to a project by negotiating the optimal cost, but only if they are brought into the project management process early on.

Further, a lot of projects have not been able to be delivered on time because the lead-time for procurement wasn't considered. Ensure you bring the appropriate materials management or procurement resource into your project during the initiation stage.

Different organizations have different approaches to dealing with procurement; from a very formal and centralized process, in which the contracting office plays a key role, to one in which the Project Manager has complete discretion. From a project planning perspective, it is important to understand how the organization handles procurement, and to incorporate the defined process, not the project plans.

Several factors can be considered in the make or buy decision including:

- Does your organization have the capability or expertise necessary for successful results?
- Does your organization want to share the risk?
- Who can do it faster, cheaper, or better?
- Does your organization want to undertake the ongoing expense of hiring a full-time staff for a discrete, short-term effort?

There are many considerations related to procurement that go beyond the selection process, including:

- What type of contracts will be used?
- What are the evaluation criteria to select outside contracts?
- What responsibilities does the Project Manager have in the procurement process?
- Are standardized procurement processes or documents used? If so, what are they?
- How will the multiple providers be managed?
- How will procurement be coordinated with the rest of the project?

How do we Plan for Quality?

Quality often gets lost in light of the other constraints; time and budget. To minimize the risk of not meeting quality standards, it is important to build quality control and quality assurance into the project costs and schedule. Quality should be planned into a project with the appropriate criteria and acceptance testing.

The primary objective of quality planning is to determine which standards apply and which metric to use to measure compliance.

The Project Manager and team must

- Clarify quality policy direction
- Determine project standards and metrics
- Understand the difference between project management process quality and technical quality

End of

PROJECT PLANNING

Stay Out of the Penalty Box!

In hockey if you have broken a rule you must stay out of the game for at least 2 minutes.

In project management making false claims, and promising delivery dates you cannot keep or did not analyze properly will result in losing your creditability.

We have developed a workable scheme to accomplish the business need(s) addressed by the project at this point!

Chapter 4:

4.0 Project Execution/Control

Questions to Answer

1. What are the Benefits Derived from Monitoring Projects?
2. How do I Manage my Own Time in a Multiple Project Environment?
3. How do I Manage Effective and Efficient Project Meetings?
4. How do we Develop a Status Report?
5. How do we Manage Project Changes (Scope Creep)?
6. How do we Deal with Conflicts?
7. How do I Develop a Communication Management Plan?
8. What do I Need to Consider when Setting Up a Project Office?

Improve Your Skating Ability

Players can have the best slap shot in the world and not make the team if they cannot master skating.

As a project manger you may have the best plan but will not be able to deliver on time and in budget if you do not have an implementation process and controls.

PROJECT EXECUTION =

Executing Processes are those that are specific to the type of project or industry

CONTROLLING =

Controlling Processes involve monitoring and measuring progress, taking corrective action when necessary

Project Execution/Control Introduction

Execution and controlling processes happen at the same time so they should be considered together.

Execution is based on the project team members performing work as per the scope statement and WBS. Remember, what is not written in the scope statement and WBS is considered <u>OUT OF SCOPE WORK!</u>

Controlling processes are managed by the Project Manager who is responsible for leading and managing changes, driving issues and communicating effectively to all stakeholders during the implementation of the WBS.

To be meaningful during the life of the project, you must keep the project plan up-to-date. It must reflect current reality. The degree of control is dependent upon:

Project Size	The larger the project, the greater the need for control.
Project Duration	The longer the project the greater the need for control.
Resource Utilization	The greater the number of staff, the greater the need for control.
Use of External Resources	The greater the use of staff from other divisions and organizations, the greater the need for control.
Size of Budget	The greater the budget, the greater the need for control.
Risk Factor	The greater the risk (seriousness, urgency, growth), the greater the need for control.

Quality / Quantity	The greater the need for quality and/or quantity, the greater the need for control.
Performance Appraisal	The less impact the project results have on the individual's performance appraisal, the greater the need for control.
Communication	The less communication amongst team members and between the Project Manager and the team members, the greater the need for control.
Schedule	The fuzzier the schedule, the greater the need for control.
Planning	Less planning means a greater need for control.
Team Member Involvement	The lower the involvement of team members in project planning, setting of objectives/output, etc., the greater the need for control.

What are the Benefits Derived from Monitoring Projects?

Project monitoring keeps the project's performance close to the project action plan by:

- Coordinating and expediting planning, analyzing what-if scenarios
- Developing better troubleshooting procedures
- Cutting costs and protecting the established schedule
- Reducing idle time to a minimum
- Tightening time scales when possible
- Using time to the advantage of the project (routine decisions made quickly - complex ones get more time)

For every project, you must monitor the following:

- The status of work being performed compared to the plan
- The estimate of remaining work based on team members' feedback
- The volume of work being completed
- The quality of work being performed
- Costs and expenditures compared to the plan
- Attitudes of people working on the project and others who are involved with the project, including customers and management
- Cohesiveness and cooperation of team members

How do I Manage my own Time in a Multiple Project Environment?

Although we have all heard the principles of time management, have attended a course, watched a DVD, or read a book, there seems to be a significant opportunity for improvement on how individuals manage their time in a project management environment.

The following four steps should apply to time management.

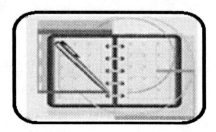

1. Dust off your planning tool

2. List your tasks in your planning tool daily; obtain these tasks not only from the Urgent – your job and high priority projects, but also from the Important – personal, life long and short term goals

3. Prioritize tasks each day

4. Review tasks each day

When working with project team members and project managers, they've expressed to me, "we've no time to do this and the schedule changes too often".

Perhaps they start work with the best intention to lay out a plan, but stuff starts hitting the fan immediately. At the end of the day, they find they weren't able to accomplish anything on their mental list. And then they discover at the end of the year, the things that mattered most may not have been accomplished!

Often, we define New Year's resolutions but we say at the end of the year, "Wow, I was pulled this way by my spouse, that way by my children, this way by my job and I didn't have time to do what matters most." Moving the clock forward 10 years could still result in the same dialogue.

Therefore, it's important to take a look at the strategic planning pyramid from a personal perspective as well. Define your own personal mission or your family mission.

Define specific and measurable deliverables that you would like to accomplish on a yearly basis and then ensure on a quarterly, monthly, and daily basis your prioritized, to-do plan consists of activities, not only from your projects, not only from your job, but also from your personal goals.

For example, if you have a goal of getting an advanced degree, it may need to be one course at a time, and a physical fitness goal may begin with one workout at a time.

And we all know how we eat an elephant – one bite at a time!

Take your plans from large Gantt charts posted on the wall, sequenced down to a daily basis of what you want to accomplish.

Prioritize those items and leave a certain portion of your daily time open to put out fires – specific percentages will vary per individual, per goal.

There is an interesting well known story that is worth reflecting upon when things in your life seem almost too much to handle, when 24 hours in a day are not enough, which is as follows:

A professor stood before his philosophy class and had some items in front of him. When the class began, he wordlessly picked up a very large and empty mayonnaise jar and proceeded to fill it with golf balls. He then asked the students if the jar was full. They agreed that it was.

The professor then picked up a box of pebbles and poured them into the jar. He shook the jar lightly. The pebbles rolled into the open areas between the golf balls. He then asked the students again if the jar was full. They agreed that it was.

The professor next picked up a box of sand and poured it into the jar. Of course, the sand filled up everything else. He asked once more if the jar was full. The students responded with a unanimous 'yes'.

The professor then produced two beers from under the table and poured the entire contents into the jar effectively filling the empty space between the sand. The students laughed.

'Now,' said the professor as the laughter subsided, 'I want you to recognize that this jar represents your life. The golf balls are the important things---your family, your children, your health, your friends and your favorite passions---and if everything else was lost and only they remained, your life would still be full.

The pebbles are the other things that matter like your job, your house and your car. The sand is everything else---the small stuff.

'If you put the sand into the jar first,' he continued, 'there is no room for the pebbles or the golf balls. The same goes for life. If you spend all your time and energy on the small stuff you will never have room for the things that are important to you.

'Pay attention to the things that are critical to your happiness. Spend time with your children. Spend time with your parents. Visit with grandparents. Take your spouse out to dinner. Play another 18 holes of golf. There will always be time to clean the house and fix the disposal. Take care of the golf ball first---the things that really matter. Set your priorities. The rest is just sand.'

One of the students raised her hand and inquired what the Beer represented. The professor smiled and said, 'I'm glad you asked.' The beer just shows you that no matter how full your life may seem, there's always room for a couple of beers with a friend.'

How do I Manage Effective and Efficient Project Meetings?

When teaching project management courses I often ask the participants how many people have attended a meeting in the last 10 days? There's usually 100% response indicating, indeed, they did attend at least one meeting. Asking the next question – "Could that meeting have been more effective and/or efficient?" Again, there's 100% response of 'yes'.

Meetings are necessary in the project management environment, and they can be run very efficiently.

Over the years, my clients have shared with me interesting, although not always practical ideas, to start a meeting on time. Some suggested keys to conducting an effective and efficient meeting, have included:

- One client meets regularly with six people but the sixth person who arrives gets a broken chair, so he or she is meeting at a much lower level than the rest.

- Another client meets regularly with eight people. Before the meeting starts someone visits a donut shop and buys a half a dozen donuts. So the last two people coming in the door don't get a donut.

- While working with a Lieutenant Colonel in the Marines, he insisted his meetings are half an hour long, period. If they're more than half an hour, the next meeting is done standing up, outside – regardless of the weather!

- Another client shared with me frustration over meetings not starting on time so they started charging $1.00 per minute for every minute a person was late to the meeting. Mind you, they had a great Christmas party, as the late fees paid for shrimp, lobster, beer, and champagne.

- Speaking of costs, a client was frustrated that the meetings were lasting far too long with far too many participants. They put a device into the meeting room where you had to swipe your card through the device. It started working like a taxi-cab meter showing the costs per minute for the meeting.

- Yet another client shared the concept of an ice-bucket meeting where they put a bucket of ice in the middle of the meeting room table and when you were talking, you had to stick your arm in the ice. You could not remove your arm until you finished speaking. People stopped monopolizing the meetings.

It is necessary with every project to have regular and efficient meetings. The following steps help to ensure successful project meetings:

- Issue an agenda in advance
- Indicate and manage the start and end times
- Add non-agenda items that arise during the meeting to a Parking Lot
- Allocate the appropriate resources
- Ensure required interests and technology are prepared in advance (Murphy's Law)
- List action items with dates and responsibilities
- The first item of the following meeting is to follow-up on all action items

Ben Duffy

Have you ever been in a situation where the meeting was going no-where, but you're not the highest ranking individual in the room and can't jump up and set the agenda?

There's a proven technique, called the "Ben Duffy" that will help you under those circumstances. It will also provide you a tool to start a meeting at any time or to break the ice when having to do requirements gathering.

It's named after the founder, Ben Duffy. He owned a small advertising firm in Atlanta, Georgia in the 1960's. He learned a major tobacco firm in New York was looking for a new agency. By luck, Ben won the opportunity to present his firm as a candidate for this work. He flew to the Big Apple, but instead of catching a Rangers game or going to see a Broadway show, Ben stayed in his room and brainstormed out questions he felt the President of the cigarette company would have about Ben, their capabilities and experience, etc.

Ben came up with 100 questions. He narrowed the list down to 10 questions. When it was Ben's turn to present, instead of doing a dog and pony show, he said to the President, "Sir, I put myself in your shoes and came up with a list of questions I thought you might have. Would you mind if we start the meeting by reviewing these questions?" The President said, "Excellent idea, Ben. I also have a list of 10 questions. Shall we compare lists?" Seven of the 10 questions matched. Ben went on to answer them effectively and to win the account.

The following summarizes the steps for a Ben Duffy technique that you could employ to either turn a meeting around or to start any given meeting, and as well to break the ice when gathering requirements.

Step 1. Put yourself in the shoes of the people you're meeting with.

Step 2. Come up with a list of questions you think they might have.

Step 3. Tell them what you do.

Step 4. Ask if you can review the questions.

Step 5. Review the questions – all at once. Set the agenda.

Step 6. Ask if there are any more questions. If there are, add them.

Step 7. Proceed to answer the questions effectively.

Consider making your first questions,

- "Who am I?"
- "What is our department?"
- "What are the objectives of the project?"

You may find you can break the ice significantly with those parties from which you need to gather requirements, because they may be thinking, "what does this person want?"; "is their project going to make my job redundant?" You may find required information isn't flowing unless you have given thought to these concerns and answered them upfront.

How do we Develop a Status Report?

In twenty plus years of consulting, I've never had a client say to me, "Mr. Wilson, we've received too many status reports."

A key to good status reports is to proactively do them. I would recommend weekly reporting.

The second key is to automate the process. We all know that doing status reports is not a lot of fun. Any opportunity to automate by connecting your status reports to your Microsoft® Office Project schedule is very efficient.

The third key is to red flag issues by ensuring the issues are prioritized.

A lot of my clients have used the stop-light approach: red, yellow, green or the rainbow report or a RAG report: red, amber, green. Either way, the key is to red flag issues. The consequences of not red flagging the hot issues can be detrimental.

One of my clients had an opportunity to bundle their technology with a major media player. About thirty days into the process, the compression technology president called me for a status report. We were not managing the project, so I didn't have access to any updates. But I made an enquiry of the media player company. They indicated they expected the integrated technology right away. In following up with the project manager, she told me that it wasn't possible because the purchase order for the testing environment was still on the CFO's desk. I asked if it was already built and integrated and she said no, as the resources were deployed elsewhere by the president himself.

The bottom line – that company is no longer in existence. But if the Project Manager had red flagged the hot issues and the executives had the intelligence to act on the red issues, perhaps they would still be in business.

Prepare good status reports by;

1) Proactively doing them weekly
2) Automate the development process, and
3) Red flag the hot issues

Status Report Checklists

- What work has been completed since the last report?

- Are there any changes to the plan?

- What issues / problems occurred since the last report?

- What actions are being taken to resolve the issues / problems?

- What are the issues that need to be resolved? (Red, Yellow, Green)

- What approvals are required?

- What work is planned for the next period?

- Who should receive this report?

- When will the next report be completed?

Example Status Report Format

Date	Project	Version

Accomplishments: % Complete per Milestone

Next Week's Tasks:

Issues:

   RED

   YELLOW

   GREEN

How do we Manage Project Changes (Scope Creep)?

The lack of project change control is one of the top five reasons why projects fail. It is not change in scope that causes failure, but the lack of change control. So before proceeding, make sure you have a scope document with SMART deliverables. Without this you cannot introduce change control. If possible, push back to the change requester to have him or her indicate any impact to the SMART deliverables and other appropriate data about the change.

Changes can also impact the overall vision or objectives of a project. For example, let's say you are commissioned to build a small bungalow. The customer may request to put an in-law or nanny suite in the back yard. They may have a budget, you may have the available resources, and you may agree upon the schedule and cost slippage.

Then a change is suggested to take the nanny suite and put it on the top floor. This is no longer a bungalow – the change has affected the whole project and there's a consequence of making the change, which would involve another risk analysis. There may also be consequences of not making the change.

Some changes are necessary. For example, one of my clients out-sourced the development of a website. Over the same 60 day period, the president changed the mission, vision and direction of the company considerably. Despite that, they didn't update the content, and put the site live sending the wrong message to all shareholders.

Also, ensure the change is approved by key stakeholders. If the change is not approved, don't just throw it away. Log it and then roll all of the changes that didn't make it in this release or version, into the next project.

A change is any deviation from an approved project plan:

- Scope (Deliverables)
- Schedule
- Costs
- Benefits

A process to manage project change requests is essential, such as the following four steps:

1. Scope with SMART Deliverables

2. Process for Collecting and Approving Changes,

      Capture / Determine:

          SMART Description of the Change

          Impact on Schedule, Resources, Costs

          Available Budget

          Impact on the Project's Vision

          Consequences of not making the Changes

3. Approve and Incorporate into Revised Plan

4. Log Changes

4. Log Changes

How do we Deal with Conflicts?

Every project manager has to spend a fair bit of time dealing with conflict. With respect to the science side of project management, you can utilize tools like Microsoft® Office Project to see if there's a conflict with resource and over-allocation.

But the art side of project management is necessary where people are not getting along or there are other issues that are escalated to you as a project manager.

Practice the following five steps that are indicated in the acronym, LSGPA.

1. **Listen** – listen for meaning. Perhaps a team member comes to your office and he feels that he is over-allocated because he is now assigned to Mary's project as well.

2. **Share** concern – get yourself on the same team as the team member by saying, "If I was in your shoes, I would feel the same way."

3. **Gain** agreement - not on the solution but on the conflict or issue. At this point you're attempting to get all 52 cards face-up on the table, saying things like, "Bob, is the fact that you're allocated to Mary's project the only thing that is preventing you from completing the task that I've assigned to you?" If he says 'yes', then "my dog ate it" or "the server crashed" – all those other excuses are now off the table.

4. **Present** your **Point**. Now you can indicate the task assigned is on the critical path and the consequences on the overall project's end-date if Bob slips on his task.

5. The last step is **Ask** for agreement on the action items. Perhaps you can say, "Bob, it's important to meet with Mary and see if we can achieve a resolution good for everyone."

Unfortunately, most Project Managers start with the "**P**" in this five-step process and present their Point and start arguing with the project team member.

Instead, follow the five steps of LSGPA.

Let's Stop Getting People Angry

Listen

Share concern

Gain Agreement

Present Your Point

Ask for agreement on Action Items

Conflict Resolution Checklist

	Yes	No
Reason for conflict is known:		
- Responsibility without authority?		
- Temporary structure vs. ongoing?		
- Existing policies & procedures?		
- Manpower, functional need vs. project need?		
- Priorities?		
- Scheduling?		
- Administration?		
- Increased costs?		
- Availability of equipment and facilities?		
Is the conflict detrimental to relationship?		
Is the ultimate objective in jeopardy?		
Is all the relevant information (including the feelings of the parties) known?		
Is this information known to all involved?		
Is a systematic approach to managing conflicts already available, including follow-up?		
Are timing and climate suitable?		
Is knowledge of the organization sufficient?		
Are the elements necessary to solve the conflict being obtained?		
Are effective listening skills being used?		
Are lines of communication always open?		
Are solutions actively being sought?		
Are third parties being involved?		
Are feelings dealt with the same importance as situations?		
Are attempts made to bring the conflict back to the simplest element?		

How do I Develop a Communication Management Plan?

Project managers and team members have said to me that they spend a lot of time chasing down documents, resending documents to the requesting parties and clarifying miscommunication around project documents. That all relates very well to the following poem:

There were once four people named: Everybody, Somebody, Anybody and Nobody.

There was an important task/job to be done, and Everybody was sure Somebody would do it.

Anybody could have done it, but Nobody did it.

Somebody got angry about that, because it was Everybody's job.

Everybody thought Anybody could do it.

It ended up that Everybody blamed Somebody when Nobody did what Anybody could have done.

The Communication Management Plan describes the communication needs of project stakeholders: who needs what information, when they will need it, and how it will be given to them.

A standard Communication Management Plan addresses internal and external project communication. It describes the methods for using and storing project information. Two factors influence communications within projects: the complexity and the environment. It is essential to plan for communication links to and between the following groups:

- Other Project Managers
- Component Managers
- Project Team Contributors
- Customers
- Management Team
- Suppliers / Vendors

Completing a Communication Management Plan

Brainstorm the anticipated communication mechanisms needed during the project and list them in the first column of the matrix.

Get approval on the completed Communication Management Plan from project stakeholders as part of the review and approval of the entire Project Management Plan. The following graphic illustrates a communication plan.

Project:						
WHO	WHAT	WHY	HOW	WHEN	WHO	WHERE
Initiator	Type of Communication	Message/ Objective	Medium	Time or Frequency	Audience	Storage	Escalation Process

What do I Need to Consider when Setting Up a Project Office?

Project Management Office (PMO) Overview

The PMO standardizes project management disciplines throughout the organization and provides guidance to the organization's Project Managers, resulting in successful project implementation. The PMO supports stakeholders through the four step process, with tools and forms, expertise, coaching, tracking and reporting, facilitation support for project review meetings, training, schedule coordination, communication, and best practices development and documentation.

Services include:

1. Guiding the organization in improving project management capability and maturity by maintaining internal and external communication

2. Seeking out best practices and opportunities for improvement

3. Supporting a consistent and repeatable project management process through centralized information, research, training, mentoring, and guidance

4. Creating an association of people who are skilled in the art and science of project management to facilitate networking and mutual support throughout the organization

PMO Roles and Responsibilities

1. Assists Project Manager with presenting new project requests and change requests for current projects for approval

2. Consolidates all project reports for the IT Management

3. Assists in creating project baseline in Microsoft Project for approved projects

4. Tracks and reports the overall program status, cross-dependencies, and risks

5. Provides access to relevant project information and materials

6. Provides Project Management Tools support

7. Administers PM documentation management and version control, Project Management Plans, templates, and form

8. Maintains Project Archives

9. Keeps the PMO Handbook current and relevant through updates and revisions

10. Facilitates PM workshops

PMO Work Flow

Project Initiation

- Assist Project Managers in developing the project scope, brainstorming, and project mapping

- Support Project Manager in presenting new project vision statements to executive project review board for review and approval

- Coordinate the development of additional information for approval, if required

Project Design (Plan)

- Assist Project Managers in developing a project Risk Analysis using brainstorming and project mapping

- Assist Project Managers in creating detailed plans, including Work Packages, Stages, Tasks, Milestones, Duration Estimates, Dependencies, and Resource Assignments

- Support the Project Manager in presenting new project risk analysis and budget plans to management for review and approval

Project Execution/Control

- Ensure the necessary tools and licenses are available so the Project Managers can maintain/update their plans

- Ensure the tools are in place to administer project change requests and controls

- Monitor the status reporting function to ensure adherence to project management procedures and timely/accurate completion

- Facilitate weekly meetings to review the active project status reports and change requests for current projects

Project Assessment/Close

- Ensure that project evaluations and lessons learned documents are submitted to PMO for each completed project

- Creates new Microsoft Project templates from completed projects, if they are repeatable and appropriate

- Ensure all the project documentation is archived in a secure, central accessible location

End of
Project Execution/Control

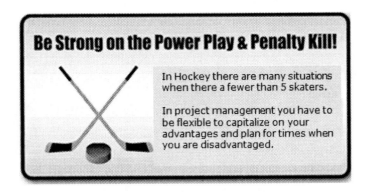

You have now developed a Scope Document and created Risk, Communication, Procurement, and Quality Plans.

Built and managed a detailed Schedule.

Managed your own time; effective meetings; and change.

Submitted weekly status reports.

You are ready to close the project.

Chapter 5:
5.0 Project Closing

Questions to Answer

1. How do we Establish Project Management Evaluation Procedures?

2. How do we Manage Project Documents?

3. What are the Project Close Steps?

4. How do we Document the Project Lessons Learned?

5. How do we Evaluate Projects?

Project Assess/Close Introduction

PROJECT CLOSING =

Acceptance of the project or stage and bringing it to an orderly end

At this point, you've developed a Project Scope Statement with SMART deliverables. You've put together the risk analysis and managed the risks well. You've developed a Project Schedule, delivered on-time and in budget. You've managed all your project communications, documentations, and meetings very effectively. You delivered your weekly status reports. You managed the inevitable change and you ran effective and efficient meetings. You are bringing the project home, on-time and in budget.

But you don't just merely walk away. There are a number of closing steps that are introduced in this chapter.

How do we Establish Project Management Evaluation Procedures?

Consider the following when considering evaluating a project:

- Have you defined SMART deliverables?
- How will you measure progress on the project?
- What kind of information do you need to assess progress?
- What standards will be used for evaluating the quality of project deliverables?

Although addressing this topic in the close section, prior to implementation, it is advisable to agree on the project evaluation methods during the planning stage.

How do we Manage Project Documents?

The end of a project is the wrong time to start to gather and archive project documentation. Prior to implementation, ask the following questions:

- What needs to be documented and archived? (Answer — The outputs at each step in the Project Management Life Cycle)

- Who is going to be responsible for documentation management? Where are you going to store the documentation? What does your Communication Plan contain?

What are the Project Close Steps?

The **Close** stage involves evaluating and documenting the project's performance and realization of benefits. It also provides recommendations that might affect or assist future projects.

The closing process formalizes project acceptance, bringing it to an orderly end. Deliverables may include:

- Metrics on performance and process improvement
- Final status meeting
- Project evaluation
- The Project performance summary, with a focus on lessons learned
- Action item closure
- Issues closure
- Contract administration closure
- Archival of project documentation
- Team recognition and reward ending the project

T Tie

U Up

L Loose

E's Ends

How do we Document the Project Lessons Learned?

1. Review Topic List

2. Modify (Add/Subtract) and Prioritize Topics

3. Create Workgroups and Divide Topics

4. Create Outline with Best Practices and Challenges for Each Topic

5. Present Findings to the Group

How Do We Evaluate Projects?

Each project is a learning experience for all resources. Verify that your S.M.A.R.T goals were met. Take time to analyze all the steps of project management and determine what went right and what went wrong using the following checklist:

① Not satisfactory

② Poor

③ Satisfactory

④ Very good

⑤ Excellent

Objectives attained and resources utilized

① ② ③ ④ ⑤

Target dates and costs met

① ② ③ ④ ⑤

Risk identified upfront

① ② ③ ④ ⑤

Responsiveness to user needs

① ② ③ ④ ⑤

Quality adequate

① ② ③ ④ ⑤

Deficiencies and problems solved

① ② ③ ④ ⑤

Realization of benefits

① ② ③ ④ ⑤

Then develop a list of recommendations to assist future projects.

End of

Project Assess/Close

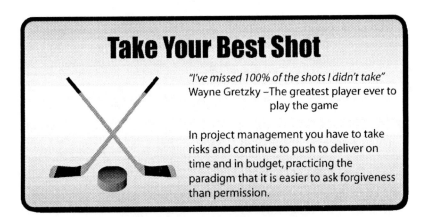

Take Your Best Shot

"I've missed 100% of the shots I didn't take"
Wayne Gretzky –The greatest player ever to
play the game

In project management you have to take
risks and continue to push to deliver on
time and in budget, practicing the
paradigm that it is easier to ask forgiveness
than permission.

Thank your team.

Prepare for the next project leveraging the lessons learned from this successful project.

Appendix A – Definitions

A **Deliverable** is the specific result of the work performed, usually based on a clearly defined Work Breakdown Structure (WBS). It is the actual project result. A project usually has both a **final deliverable** and **interim deliverables**. The customer may or may not receive the interim deliverables, but they are required to achieve the final deliverable.

Project **Milestones** are significant completion points during a project. Milestones have zero duration and may or may not have a deliverable attached. They communicate status and track progress more effectively.

A **Project** is a temporary endeavor undertaken to create a unique product or service. Every project has an end.

The **Project Manager (PM)** is the primary leader, communicator, coordinator, and champion for a project. The PM is a temporary position, selected from within the organization early in the project life cycle.

The **Project Stakeholders** are those most impacted by the project and who have an interest in its outcome. They may include the people who establish project deliverables and constraints and implement the strategies and schedules. For example, project stakeholders may include project sponsors, project managers, line managers, team members, customers (internal and external), outside agencies, and vendors.

The **Project Team** is a temporary group, formed to accomplish a specific project. The team disbands when the project is completed.

A **Scope Statement** is a clear and concise written document that includes the project description in terms of what, where, and when, along with a list of expected results. It is the major component of the project and it forms the basis of an agreement and shared vision for all project stakeholders.

A **Task** is the lowest level of schedule detail. It is a manageable description of work with estimated duration, dependencies with other tasks (which define the critical path), and resource assignments. Progress tracking occurs at the task level by recording percentage complete, actual dates/duration, and actual hours/cost.

A **Template** is a Microsoft Project plan that contains standard tasks for a new project.

A **Work Package** is a group of related tasks organized to achieve a specific milestone, which is generally an interim deliverable toward the successful production of the project's final deliverable(s).

A **Work Breakdown Structure (WBS)** is a hierarchical organization of the work necessary to complete the project. A WBS consists of work packages, stages, tasks, milestones, and deliverables. It is the foundation for building a new project schedule. The WBS information populates the Task Name column in Microsoft Project. The WBS is a derivative of the Scope/Vision Statement. Together, the Scope/Vision Statement and WBS constitute the total project Scope/Vision.

Appendix B – The Sports Bag

A Graphical Summary of the equipment/tools illustrated in the

The Project Management Play Book - It's A Team Sport

I D E A

=

Success vs. Failure – The Bottom Line

Success = Met Expectations

Failure = Unmet Expectations

Successful projects require:
- Clear alignment with business goals and strategies
- "Project Governance" - Vocal sponsorship and active guidance from Business Owners
- Funding and committed resources

The Strategic Planning Pyramid illustrates the importance of connecting your projects to strategic initiatives or long-term goals and in turn, the mission.

Strategic Planning Pyramid

Project Mapping

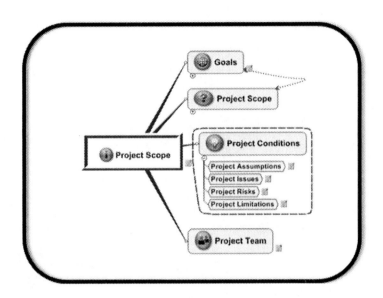

Key Stakeholder

W Willingness

O Optimism

M Money/Means

A Authority

N Need

Baseball - Requirements Gathering

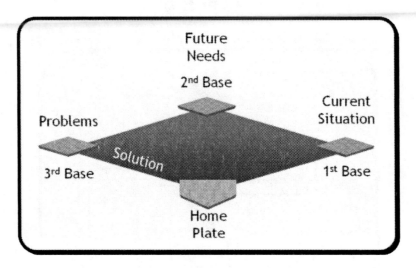

Questioning Funnel

Ensure your scope statement is S.M.A.R.T.

Specific

Measurable

Achievable

Relevant

Time Constrained

Three types of questions illustrated in the questioning Funnel and Scale diagram

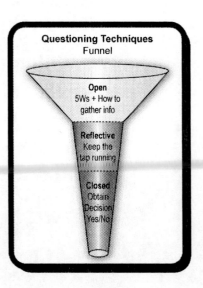

Questioning Scale

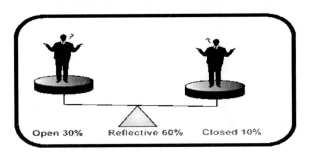

Open 30%   Reflective 60%   Closed 10%

Project Planning Steps

1. Review Scope Statement
2. Determine Dominating Factors – Triple Constraint
3. Define and Quantify Risks
4. Develop the Work Breakdown Structure
    a. Determine Phases/Activities
    b. Determine Project Tasks
    c. Set the Milestones
5. Determine the Task Duration
6. Sequence the Activities for Efficiency and Logical Connections
7. Identify the Critical Path
8. List the Project Resources
9. Assign Resources to Tasks
10. Optimize the Plan
11. Produce Reports and Communicate the Plan
12. Review the Feasibility of the Project (time, cost, scope, quality, risks)
13. Document Assumptions and Issues (ongoing throughout process)
14. Obtain Approval of the Plan
15. Freeze the Plan (set the baseline)

117

Triple Constraints

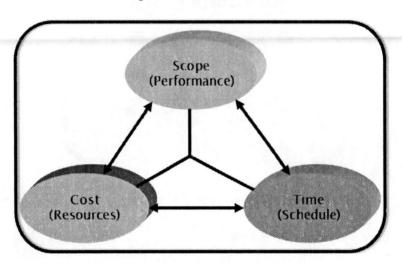

Risk Assessment

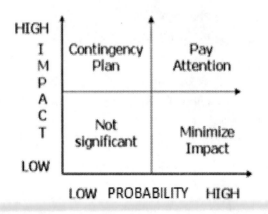

Risk	Impact	Probability	Weight	Avoidance/ Contingency	Resource
	1-5	%			Responsible

Work Break Down Stucture

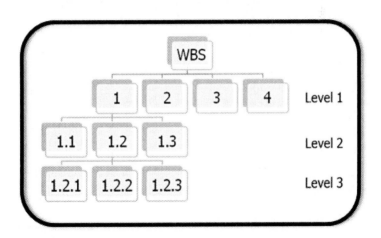

Communication Plan

	Project:						
WHO	**WHAT**	**WHY**	**HOW**	**WHEN**	**WHO**	**WHERE**	
Initiator	Type of Communication	Message/ Objective	Medium	Time or Frequency	Audience	Storage	Escalation Process

Final Schedule Checklist

Assumptions	No assumptions are violated
Critical Path	Clearly marked on the network diagram
Consensus	All major participants have reviewed dates for completeness and accuracy
Dates	All holidays and special events have been noted appropriately; no resource conflicts exist
Chart	Clearly specifies tasks, durations, individual responsibilities, and target start and finish dates
Slack	The plan contains adequate slack and fudge.

Ben Duffy

Step 1. Put yourself in the shoes of the people you're meeting with.
Step 2. Come up with a list of questions you think they might have.
Step 3. Tell them what you did.
Step 4. Ask if you can review the questions.
Step 5. Review the questions – all at once. Set the agenda.
Step 6. Ask if there are any more questions. If there are, add them.
Step 7. Proceed to answer the questions effectively.

Status Report Checklists

- What work has been completed since the last report?

- Are there any changes to the plan?

- What problems occurred since the last report?

- What actions are being taken to resolve the problems?

- What are the issues that need to be resolved? (Red, Orange, Green)

- What approvals are required?

- What work is planned for the next period?

- Who should receive this report?

- When will the next report be completed?

Example Status Report Format

Date   Project   Version

Accomplishments

% Complete per Milestone

Next Week's Tasks

Issues

  RED

  YELLOW

  GREEN

How do we Manage Project Changes (Scope Creep)?

1. Scope with SMART Goals
2. Process for Collecting and Approving Changes,

      Capture/Determine:

         SMART Description of the Change

         Impact on Schedule, Resources, Costs

         Budget Available

         Impact on the Project's Vision

         Consequences of not making the Change

3. Approve and Incorporate into Revised Plan
4. Log Changes

Conflict Resolution

Let's Stop Getting People Angry

Listen
Share concern
Gain Agreement
Present Your Point
Ask for agreement on Action Items

	Yes	No
Reason for conflict is known:		
- Responsibility without authority?		
- Temporary structure vs. ongoing?		
- Existing policies & procedures?		
- Manpower, functional need vs. project need?		
- Priorities?		
- Scheduling?		
- Administration?		
- Increased costs?		
- Availability of equipment and facilities?		
Is the conflict detrimental to relationship?		
Is the ultimate objective in jeopardy?		
Is all the relevant information (including the feelings of the parties) known?		
Is this information known to all involved?		
Is a systematic approach to managing conflicts already available, including follow-up?		
Are timing and climate suitable?		
Is knowledge of the organization sufficient?		
Are the elements necessary to solve the conflict being obtained?		
Are effective listening skills being used?		
Are lines of communication always open?		
Are solutions actively being sought?		
Are third parties being involved?		
Are feelings dealt with the same importance as situations?		
Are attempts made to bring the conflict back to the simplest element?		

T   Tie

U   Up

L   Loose

Es Ends

Project Evaluation

Rnakings

    ① Not satisfactory

    ② Poor

    ③ Satisfactory

    ④ Very good

    ⑤ Excellent

Objectives attained and resources utilized

① ② ③ ④ ⑤

Target dates and costs met

① ② ③ ④ ⑤

Risk identified`

① ② ③ ④ ⑤

Responsiveness to user needs

① ② ③ ④ ⑤

Quality adequate

① ② ③ ④ ⑤

Deficiencies and problems solved

① ② ③ ④ ⑤

Realization of benefits

① ② ③ ④ ⑤

Appendix C

The Project Management Play Book - It's a Team Sport

Project Management Forms

I D E A

Phase	Initiation		
Document	**Key Stakeholder Interview Form**	**SMART Goals Guidelines**	**Project Scope Document**
Purpose	Document the Need for a project from the Key Stakeholder's point of view	Explains how to document Goals in SMART terms (Specific, Measurable, Attainable, Relevant, and Time Dimensioned)	Converts an idea, policy and/or strategic initiative into the details of a potential project.
PHASE	Design/Planning		
Document	**WBS (using Microsoft Project Template)**	**Project Communication Plan**	**Risk Assessment**
Purpose	Initially documents tasks, generic resources, and duration. Provides a cost breakdown for further use in future documentation.	Documents the process and frequency of project communication.	Documents risks, their probability, impact, mitigation strategy, and assignment.

PHASE	Executing and Controlling				
Document	**Change Request Form**	**Status Reports**	**Meeting Planner**	**Milestone Acceptance Document**	**WBS Baseline**
Purpose	Documents requested changes to the project as it progresses. All changes to the project must be formally accepted by the Key Stakeholder(s) before the change will be made.	Regular communications to ensure all parties are aware of project progress.	Document used to plan project meetings	Documents formal acceptance of completed milestones by the Key Stakeholder(s).	The 'road map' used by the Project Team to deliver the agreed project deliverables.

127

PHASE	Assess/Closing		
Document	Project Evaluation Worksheet	Project Review Report	Project Acceptance Document
Purpose	This worksheet is used to evaluate the progress of the project.	Documents the project's successes and failures. It is completed after the Lessons Learned meeting. This document also details how the project deliverables are utilized by the department(s) to realize the SMART Goals.	Documents formal acceptance of the completed project by the Key Stakeholder(s).

1.0 Project Key Stakeholder Interview Form

Project Name:	
Key Stakeholder:	Today's Date:
Department:	

How would you characterize the need for the proposed project?
What SMART goals would you like the project to fulfill? What are the goal priorities?
Do you know what departments will be impacted by this proposed project? If so, what are they?
Is there a Strategic Initiative(s) in which this project is related?
What would you include in this project?
What would you exclude from this project?
Do you know of any barriers to the proposed project?

SMART Goal Development Guidelines

Project goals are to be documented using SMART criteria. Below is a definition of the acronym:

S	**Specific**
M	**Measurable**
A	**Attainable**
R	**Relevant**
T	**Time Dimensioned and Specific**

Goals should be specific so that everyone is aware of exactly what is to be achieved.

Measurable
Goals must be measurable so that we know when they have been reached.

Attainable
Can we complete the project? Goals should be examined to determine if they are attainable during the project process.

Relevant
The Stakeholder(s) and/or the Project Manager must determine what Strategic Initiative this project will relate to and if the goal is relevant to the overall big picture.

Time Dimensioned
Goals must be documented with a specific time constraint so that the goal can be realized in a reasonable timeframe.

Examples:

Goal (without SMART criteria): Provide a more user-friendly software solution

Goal (with SMART criteria): Provide a software solution which is GUI/Windows based providing point and click functionality, with a satisfaction rating of not les that 4.5 out of 5.

2.0 Project Scope Document

Scope ID:	Today's Date:	
Project Name:	Reference Number:	
Division:	Target Finish:	
Prepared By:	Status:	

<table>
<tr><th colspan="2">One Time Project Costs</th></tr>
<tr><th>Category</th><th>CostS</th></tr>
<tr><td>Internal Staff Labor</td><td></td></tr>
<tr><td>Outside Service</td><td></td></tr>
<tr><td>Software</td><td></td></tr>
<tr><td>Hardware</td><td></td></tr>
<tr><td>Materials and Supplies</td><td></td></tr>
<tr><td>Facilities</td><td></td></tr>
<tr><td>Telecommunications</td><td></td></tr>
<tr><td>Training</td><td></td></tr>
<tr><td>Contingency</td><td></td></tr>
</table>

Recurring Costs	
Category	**Costs**
Internal Staff Labor	
Outside Service	
Software	
Hardware	
Materials and Supplies	
Facilities	
Telecommunications	
Training	
Contingency	

Project Justification (SMART Goals)

Project Product

Project Deliverables

Project Objectives

3.0 Project Risk Plan

Risk	Impact 1-5	Probability %	Weight	Avoidance/ Contingency	Resource Responsible

4.0 Project Communication Plan

Project:							
WHO	WHAT	WHY	HOW	WHEN	WHO	WHERE	
Initiator	Type of Communication	Message/ Objective	Medium	Time or Frequency	Audience	Storage	Escalation Process

5.0 Project Change Request

Complete this tool if the change meets one or more of the following criteria: The change is estimated to cost more than $_____ The change moves the schedule by more than_____%. The change alters the original project vision statement

Project Title:	Date:

Description of Change
1.Describe the proposed project change (SMART)
2. List the reasons for the proposed change
3.Identify how the change will affect the following project elements:
Project Schedule:
Cost:
Resources:
4. Does the change affect the original project goal statement? If yes, how?
5.Describe the effect on the project if this change is not made ((keep project Status quo)

Describe the Risk associated with this change.				
Risk	**Impact**	**Probability**	**Weight**	**Avoidance/ Contingency**
Accountability—Person Requesting the Change Request				
Name:			Date:	
Project Key Stakeholder(s) Approval				
Name:			Date:	

6.0 Project Status Report

Project Status Report	
Project Manager:	**Status Report Number:**
Project Name **Accomplishments:**	**Date:**
Next Steps:	
Issues: **Green**	
Yellow	
Red	

7.0 Meeting Planner

Date Scheduled:					
Meeting Title:					
Purpose:					
Desired Results:					
Location:					
Meeting Method:					
Facilitator:				**Recorder:**	
Scheduled Time			**Actual Time**		
Start:	Stop:	Total Hours:	Start:	Stop:	
Attendees			**Department**		
1.					
2.					
3.					
4.					
5.					
6.					
Items to be Discussed					
1.					
2.					
3.					
4.					

8. 0 Milestone Acceptance Document

Project Name:	
Author:	**Contact Information:**
Revision History **First Revision:**	**First Draft:** **Second Revision:**
Milestone	

What was delivered as a result of the completion of this milestone?
How was the acceptability of the milestone verified with the client?
What open items remain in regard to this milestone?
What is the plan for resolving those open items (including owners and dates)?
By signing below we acknowledge that the above milestone has been completed to our satisfaction.

Signatures

Name	Signature	Responsibility	Date

9.0 Project Evaluation Worksheet

Project Title:	
Project Manager:	
Project Start Date:	Finish Date:
On a scale of 1 to 5, rate the following areas to describe your project. **1** Very poor **2** Poor **3** Average**4** Good **5** Very good	
Initiation	**Rating**
1. The end result met original desired results.	
2. The original plan was achievable (realistic).	
3. I (we) accomplished what was actually achievable.	
4. How do others view the project?	
• Users	
• Steering Committee/Stakeholder(s)	
• Team Members	
• IT Management	
• Self (Project Manager)	
• Other	
5. Stakeholders were accurately identified.	
6. Stakeholders' desired results were understood.	
	Total:

Planning	Rating
1. The project met budget specifications.	
2. The project met timeline specifications.	
3. The project met technical specifications.	
4. Risks were clearly identified.	
5. Risks were successfully managed.	
6. The communication plan was completed and useful	
7. Adequate resources were identified	
8. Adequate Resource were available for the project	
9. Business Case was completed satisfactorily	
10. MS Project was used effectively	
	Total:

Executing	Rating
1. I (we) implemented the plan successfully.	
2. I (we) revised the plan sufficiently and expediently.	
3. Necessary resources were available.	
4. Review meetings were timely.	
5. Review meetings were managed effectively.	
6. The change Control Process was effective	
7. Microsoft Project updated using Project Server effectively	
8. Project documentation was adequate.	
9. Project documentation was updated and managed effectively.	
	Total:

Closing	Rating
1. The project ended in a timely manner.	
2. Project documentation was complete and archived.	
3. We received evaluations from all team members.	
4. The project documentation can help us identify and close the gap between time estimates and real time.	
5. The project documentation can help us identify and close the gap between estimated costs and actual costs.	
6. The SMART Goals were obtained	
7. We have the identified areas of improvements and ways to improve those areas for the next project.	
	Total:

10.0 Project Review Report

Project Name:
Reviewer(s):
Revision History   **First Review Date:**
Background to the Project
Project Review Methodology
PROJECT PERFORMANCE **Performance against SMART Goals**
Performance against Deliverables
Performance against Budget
LESSONS LEARNED
What worked well?
What could be improved?

11.0 Project Acceptance Document

Project Name:	
Author:	**Contact Information:**
Revision History	**First Draft:**
First Revision:	**Second Revision:**
Were the SMART goals realized with the completion of the project? If not, why not?	
What was delivered as a result of the completion of this project?	
How was the acceptability of the project verified with the Key Stakeholder(s), Steering Committee and IT Management?	
What open items remain in regard to this project?	
What is the plan for resolving those open items (including owners and dates)?	
By signing below we acknowledge that the above project has been completed to our satisfaction.	

Signatures

Name	Signature	Responsibility	Date

NOTES

NOTES

NOTES